Expansions of Feminist Family Theory Through Diversity

Expansions of Feminist Family Theory Through Diversity

Rhea V. Almeida
Editor

The Haworth Press, Inc.
New York • London • Norwood (Australia)

Expansions of Feminist Family Theory Through Diversity has also been published as *Journal of Feminist Family Therapy*, Volume 5, Numbers 3/4 1994.

The development, preparation, and publication of this work has been undertaken with great care. However, the publisher, employees, editors, and agents of The Haworth Press and all imprints of The Haworth Press, Inc., including The Haworth Medical Press and Pharmaceutical Products Press, are not responsible for any errors contained herein or for consequences that may ensue from use of materials or information contained in this work. Opinions expressed by the author(s) are not necessarily those of The Haworth Press, Inc.

The Haworth Press, Inc., 10 Alice Street, Binghamton, NY 13904-1580 USA

Library of Congress Cataloging-in-Publication Data

Expansions of feminist family theory through diversity / Rhea V. Almeida, editor.

     p. cm.

     "Has also been published as Journal of feminist family therapy, volume 5, numbers 3/4, 1994"–T.p. verso.

     Includes bibliographical references and index.

     ISBN 1-56024-667-7 (alk. paper).–ISBN 1-56023-063-0 (alk. paper)

     1. Family psychotherapy. 2. Feminist therapy. 3. Feminist theory. 4. Family psychotherapy–Social aspects. 5. Oppression (Psychology) I. Almeida, Rhea V.

RC488.5.E98 1994   94-175

616.89'156–dc20   CIP

DEDICATION

To Rich Ginsberg, Arielle and Lara, whose warmth and love continually provide for me.

To the memory of my mother Blanche and father Leonard.

To my grandmothers Hortulana and Nevilina.
To my grandfathers Francis and Ralph.

To all of my special friends and teachers, without whose guidance and support I could not have reached this far.

INDEXING & ABSTRACTING

Contributions to this publication are selectively indexed or abstracted in print, electronic, online, or CD-ROM version(s) of the reference tools and information services listed below. This list is current as of the copyright date of this publication. See the end of this section for additional notes.

- *Abstracts of Research in Pastoral Care & Counseling,* Loyola College, 7135 Minstrel Way, Suite 101, Columbia, MD 21045

- *Family Violence & Sexual Assault Bulletin,* Family Violence & Sexual Assault Institute, 1310 Clinic Drive, Tyler, TX 75701

- *Feminist Periodicals: A Current Listing of Contents,* Women's Studies Librarian-at-Large, 728 State Street, 430 Memorial Library, Madison, WI 53706

- *Index to Periodical Articles Related to Law,* University of Texas, 727 East 26th Street, Austin, TX 78705

- *Inventory of Marriage and Family Literature (online and hard copy),* National Council on Family Relations, 3989 Central Avenue NE, Suite 550, Minneapolis, MN 55421

- *Mental Health Abstracts (online through DIALOG),* IFI/Plenum Data Company, 3202 Kirkwood Highway, Wilmington, DE 19808

- *Social Work Abstracts,* National Association of Social Workers, 750 First Street NW, 8th Floor, Washington, DC 20002

- *Studies on Women Abstracts,* Carfax Publishing Company, P.O. Box 25, Abingdon, Oxfordshire OX14 3UE, United Kingdom

- *Women Studies Abstracts,* Rush Publishing Company, P.O. Box 1, Rush, NY 14543

(continued)

SPECIAL BIBLIOGRAPHIC NOTES

related to special journal issues (separates)
and indexing/abstracting

☐ indexing/abstracting services in this list will also cover material in the "separate" that is co-published simultaneously with Haworth's special thematic journal issue or DocuSerial. Indexing/abstracting usually covers material at the article/chapter level.

☐ monographic co-editions are intended for either non-subscribers or libraries which intend to purchase a second copy for their circulating collections.

☐ monographic co-editions are reported to all jobbers/wholesalers/approval plans. The source journal is listed as the "series" to assist the prevention of duplicate purchasing in the same manner utilized for books-in-series.

☐ to facilitate user/access services all indexing/abstracting services are encouraged to utilize the co-indexing entry note indicated at the bottom of the first page of each article/chapter/contribution.

☐ this is intended to assist a library user of any reference tool (whether print, electronic, online, or CD-ROM) to locate the monographic version if the library has purchased this version but not a subscription to the source journal.

☐ individual articles/chapters in any Haworth publication are also available through the Haworth Document Delivery Services (HDDS).

Expansions of Feminist Family Theory Through Diversity

CONTENTS

ABOUT THE EDITOR

Rhea V. Almeida, ACSW, is Founder/Director of the Institute for Family Services in Somerset, New Jersey. She is of Asian Indian descent, and grew up in Uganda and London before coming to the United States. She has written on family violence, Asian Indian families, mentoring, and unexamined assumptions in service delivery. She has served on the Gay/Lesbian Task Force for NASW and is currently on the Credentialing Board for Domestic Violence. Her special interests include: culture, gender and race in clinical training. She is on the faculty of the Family Institute of New Jersey, Metuchen, New Jersey.

Introduction

Rhea V. Almeida

Feminist analysis has raised the question: how do power and domination shape the intimate connections of men and women in families? The question embracing diversity within this evolution is: how do race, class, culture, and gender socially construct varying dimensions of social inequality that in turn organize different forms of family life?

Feminist family theory has challenged the assumptions of gender; however, the diversity of family life within race, class, and culture has remained outside of this discourse. Unlike other schools of family therapy, feminist family theory requires an examination of the therapeutic institution with regard to its role in perpetuating or changing the values and social structures oppressive to family life. Therefore, feminist family theory is best equipped to include ideas of diversity.

A large body of literature on ethnicity and culture exists, although most of it is not linked to a feminist theoretical orientation.

Rhea V. Almeida, ACSW, is Founder/Director, Institute of Family Services (IFS), Somerset, NJ and is on the Faculty, Family Institute of New Jersey, Metuchen, NJ.

The author would like to offer special recognition to many "third world" feminists whose writings remain invisible to many mainstream scholars: Paula Gunn Allen, bell hooks, Patricia Hill Collins, Audre Lorde, Cherrie Moraga, Gloria Anzaldua, Karin Aguilar-San Juan, and Mitsuye Yamada who have influenced her thinking and enabled her to see the many complex and different possibilities in family life.

[Haworth co-indexing entry note]: "Introduction." Almeida, Rhea V. Co-published simultaneously in the *Journal of Feminist Family Therapy* (The Haworth Press, Inc.) Vol. 5, No. 3/4, 1994, pp. 1-3; and: *Expansions of Feminist Family Theory Through Diversity* (ed: Rhea V. Almeida) The Haworth Press, Inc., 1994, pp. 1-3. Multiple copies of this article/chapter may be purchased from The Haworth Document Delivery Center [1-800-3-HAWORTH; 9:00 a.m. - 5:00 p.m. (EST)].

Ethnic hierarchies intertwined with class differences, cultural prejudices, and even religious biases remain relatively unchallenged.
This volume examines the conceptual link between feminist theory
and diversity. It positions issues of race, class, culture, and sexual
orientation centrally with gender.

To embrace a context that hears both historical and contemporary
experiences of oppression, societies need to possess a collective
memory of past atrocities. Remembering helps a society move out
of the process of denial. Unknotting the painful and shameful aspects of privilege and oppression in a society that claims no
memory of past atrocities creates particular dilemmas for family
therapists. Ideals of family life become mere forms of literacy to be
imposed by those in power upon the less fortunate.

The theoretical perspectives advanced in this collection provide
opportunities for rethinking the traditions expressed in many ideas
of family therapy.

Hardy and Laszloffy analyze the metalanguage of race in family
theory, training, and practice, and bring into the therapy room realities often awkwardly confronted or shamefully avoided. Comas-
Díaz furthers this analysis through her poignant descriptions of
racial oppression within the Latin communities of America and the
Caribbean. Implications for the social and personal well being of
the *LatiNegra* are offered.

In continuing the theme of societal-power imbalances replicated
within the context of family therapy, Korin explicates therapeutic
dilemmas engendered within such a context. The application of
Freire's principles suggests a new moral consciousness.

Feminist theory has challenged assumptions inherent in the public-
private distinction of family life, emphasizing the personal political
predicament of white middle-class women. An examination of *public* origins of personal exploitation in racially and sexually different
families has occupied less prominence in feminist family therapy.
This analysis of public expression is examined through the diverse
experiences of the racially and sexually different in the article by
Almeida, Woods, Messineo, Font, and Heer.

The feminist struggle represents efforts to free all families from
experiences of oppression. McGoldrick's chapter echoes this vision. While society experiences a growing intolerance for violence

against women and children, increasing support for female strength, freedom, and personal dignity, rising evidence of egalitarianism in social relationships, and an expanding critical concern for our environment, many roots of oppression remain uninvestigated. The intent of this volume is to elucidate the diverse influences of oppression that shape both the institution of family therapy as well as family life. It represents the beginning of a dialogue about our current life struggles from which we hope to all be free.

Deconstructing Race in Family Therapy

Kenneth V. Hardy
Tracey A. Laszloffy

SUMMARY. Despite the pervasive significance of race in society, attention devoted to racial issues in family therapy has been minimal. This paper explores the ways in which family therapy has relegated racial issues to a position of insignificance through a process of marginalization. Recommendations for recognizing the saliency of race within family therapy theory, practice, and training are described.

There are few issues in society that are as value-laden and misunderstood as is race. The extant confusion about race is, at least in part, attributable to the schism that exists between the biological and socio-political dimensions of race. The biological dimension is based upon an analysis of the range of genotypic and phenotypic traits that exist within the human species. This analysis has resulted in the identification of three "distinct" racial groups: Negroid, Mongoloid, and Caucasoid. These categories have been useful as biological descriptors, however their usefulness has been beclouded by socio-politically constructed meanings. The socio-political di-

Kenneth V. Hardy, PhD, is Director of Clinical Training and Research of the Marriage and Family Therapy Program at Syracuse University, 008 Slocum Hall, Syracuse, NY 13244. Tracey A. Laszloffy, MA, is a Doctoral student in the Marriage and Family Therapy Program at Syracuse University, 008 Slocum Hall, Syracuse, NY 13244.

[Haworth co-indexing entry note]: "Deconstructing Race in Family Therapy." Hardy, Kenneth V., and Tracey A. Laszloffy. Co-published simultaneously in the *Journal of Feminist Family Therapy* (The Haworth Press, Inc.) Vol. 5, No. 3/4, 1994, pp. 5-33; and: *Expansions of Feminist Family Theory Through Diversity* (ed: Rhea V. Almeida) The Haworth Press, Inc., 1994, pp. 5-33. Multiple copies of this article/chapter may be purchased from The Haworth Document Delivery Center [1-800-3-HAWORTH; 9:00 a.m. - 5:00 p.m. (EST)].

mension of race has established a relationship between membership in a particular racial group and social status, privilege, and power. For instance, members of the Caucasoid racial group have enjoyed the greatest degree of social privilege and power, while members of the Negroid and Mongoloid racial groups have experienced the least.

Skin color is but one of several physical characteristics that defines racial identity, however, it is by far the most potent. The mere presence of skin color immediately constructs racial realities that consistently shape "who" participates in a process and "how." It also significantly influences all social interactions throughout the lifecycle (e.g., where one lives, how and where one is educated, who one dates and marries, how one is buried, etc.).

The potency of skin color, like race, also is punctuated by its relationship to social privilege and power. In numerous societies there exists a social hierarchy based on skin color that rewards lighter tones and punishes darker ones. The tendency among whites to view all people of color as inferior often impairs their understanding of the ways in which the hierarchy also persists among people of color. Although whites as a collective may regard all people of color as essentially "black," among people of color a critical distinction is drawn between being "non-white" and being "black."[1]

The distinction that exists between and among people of color further reflects the complicated relationship between skin color, race, and social privilege and power. Although all people of color are subjects of prejudice and discrimination on the basis of their non-white skin, blacks are discriminated against on the basis of both skin color and race. The socially constructed nature of race is such that Caucasoid features have been defined as the ideal, therefore, Negroid features, by virtue of differing the most markedly, have been the most socially devalued. For instance, a dark complexioned Asian Indian and an African black of similar dark complexion may both be discriminated against on the basis of skin color. However, with regard to racial identity, the Asian Indian would probably be granted higher social status and privilege than the African black on the basis of phenotypical characteristics that extend beyond skin color. Despite the dark skin of the Asian Indian, the lack of Negroid-like physical features would likely afford this person an advantage with regard to the racially-based hierarchy of social privilege and power. As illustrated, skin color and race are distinct as well as inextricably interrelated phenomena.[2]

THE PROBLEM WITH TERMINOLOGY

As the aforementioned discussion highlights, many of the challenges embedded in discussing race is a function of social construction and language. Even the term "race" is problematic because of the confusion generated by its denotative and connotative meanings. Denotatively "race" refers to all racial groups: Negroid, Mongoloid, and Caucasoid. However, connotatively, it is often interpreted to mean "black people." Consider the title of this chapter, "Deconstructing Race In Family Therapy." Denotatively, the term "race" refers to the marginalization of racial issues as they relate to people of all racial groups. However, connotatively, this title may be interpreted as a reference to the marginalization of racial issues as they relate specifically to black people. Thus, the language used to describe racial issues is often confusing and woefully inadequate.[3]

The difficulty embedded in discussing racial issues is further complicated by the absence of terminology to describe racial groups other than "blacks" and "whites." Aside from the scientific terms (Negroid, Mongoloid, and Caucasoid), "black" and "white" are the only widely recognized terms for addressing racial differences in American culture. This inadequacy is obscured by the use of confusing socio-political categories such as "Hispanic" and "Asian." These politically-based descriptors becloud conceptualization and comprehension regarding distinctions between race, skin color, ethnicity, and culture. Consider the group called "Hispanic" as a means of illustrating the confusion. The term "Hispanic" is generally used to refer to people of Spanish origin. However, this seemingly monolithic group is comprised of numerous ethnic groups whose roots extend throughout much of Central and South America and parts of the Caribbean. In addition to their ethnic diversity, "Hispanics" also are characterized by considerable racial diversity as well. Therefore, "Hispanics" might be "black," "white," or "something in between," but the limitations embedded in current terminology do not allow for a cogent discussion of these racial differences.

The same argument could be advanced with regard to the term African Americans. It is assumed that this term refers to black Americans who are of African descent, however, because Africa refers to a continent, not a racial group, technically African Americans can be either "black" or "white." Thus, far from aiding our understanding of race, language often obscures it.

THE MARGINALIZATION OF RACE
IN FAMILY THERAPY

Despite the prominent role that race plays in society, its significance in family therapy is marginalized. The process of marginalization is associated closely with the myth of colorblindness–we don't see color, and a collective silence with regard to race–we don't talk about it. The phenomenon of not seeing (colorblindness) or not talking about race (silence) constructs the perception that race is irrelevant. Upon closer examination however, it becomes evident that the opposite is true. The blindness and mutism associated with race are sophisticated mechanisms that serve the purpose of obscuring the relevance of racial issues.

The marginalization of race obfuscates the comprehension of the ways in which the philosophical underpinnings of family therapy is dominated by a white perspective. This perspective pervades the ideological foundation of the field without challenge or accountability. Consequently, the ideologies of other racial groups are suppressed. As an illustration, consider the titles of the following articles: "Family-of-Origin and Family Therapy Considerations With Black Families" (1987) and "The Family Life Cycle of Poor Black Families" (1988). The titles of these articles, as well as Boyd-Franklin's "Black Families and Therapy" (1989), highlights the implicit understanding that exists with regard to racial references in family therapy. Each of the above authors understands that a lack of racial denotation translates into whites. Therefore, when referring to groups other than whites, it is necessary to include racial qualification. To further highlight this point, note that references to "Therapy With White People" do not exist in family therapy literature.

This is further evidence that when race is not explicitly denoted, the underlying assumption is that whites are the non-specified reference group. Non-whites, on the other hand, are represented only on the rare occasions when race is addressed overtly.

The following section provides a brief critique of the salient aspects of racial marginalization throughout the family therapy field.

Literature

Family therapy scholarship devotes scant attention to racial issues. Reviews of prominent family therapy journals reveal that with a few minor exceptions (e.g., Bagarrozi, 1980), articles addressing race in general, or racial minorities specifically are underrepresented. The inattention devoted to racial issues is not limited to periodicals. It also exists in family therapy books. Boyd-Franklin's book *Black Families in Therapy* (1989) is the notable exception and represents the most comprehensive work addressing black families in relation to family therapy. Although Boyd-Franklin presents variations of her book in chapter form in other family therapy books, such as *Ethnicity and Family Therapy* (McGoldrick, Pearce, & Giordano, 1982) and *Minorities and Family Therapy* (Saba, Karrer, & Hardy, 1991), few other substantive works have emerged in this area.

The marginalization of racial issues in family therapy literature is evidenced further by the paucity of attention devoted to racial minority groups other than African Americans. Although other racial minority groups (such as Asian Americans and Latinos, etc.) receive some attention in the literature, racial issues are rarely addressed specifically. The literature devoted to these groups often addresses their cultural/ethnic heritages and not their racial identities.

Theory

Prior to the 1980s, with the exception of groundbreaking work by Minuchin and Montalvo (1966, 1967), and Aponte (1974, 1976), the impact of socio-cultural factors upon families received little attention in family therapy theory. This oversight contributed to a narrow conceptualization of families based on what I have described elsewhere (Hardy, 1991) as the Theoretical Myth of Sameness (TMOS). This concept refers to an epistemological stance or worldview based on the assumption that all families are virtually the same. The "universality" of the family is thought to transcend any differences that may be attributable to factors such as race, ethnicity, and/or gender. This worldview represents a meta-framework that organizes family therapy theory and practice. Consequently, family therapy theory marginalizes the significance of race through adhering to the notion of universal principles purported to transcend racial differences.

Despite claims of universality, all theories, regardless of the measures employed to ensure their "objectivity" and "generalizability," reflect the ideological biases of their creators. This is particularly noteworthy since the majority of the family therapy theory is constructed by white, European and Euro-American males. This influence pervades the theory. For instance, family therapy theory places a high premium on patriarchal Eurocentric principles such as individualism, competition, autonomy, mastery of and control over the environment, and dualistic thinking. The patriarchical Eurocentric biases in family therapy are critiqued extensively in feminist literature (James & McIntyre, 1983; Goldner, 1985; Ault-Riché, 1986; Bograd, 1987).

The values and ideology associated with most racial minority groups are not consistent with many of the Eurocentric principles that characterize family therapy. Many non-white, non-European groups emphasize group identity, cooperation, harmony with the environment, reciprocal obligation, and holistic thinking. Oddly enough, none of these traits play an integral role in family therapy notions regarding healthy family functioning. These values are embedded deeply in the cultural traditions of many racial minority groups, and often reflect an adaptive response to racial oppression. For example, African American culture is structured around the principles of group unity, cooperation and mutual responsibility. These principles are rooted in an African philosophical heritage (Nobles, 1978), and are reinforced by the hardships imposed by slavery, as well as present day racially-based oppression.

Minimizing the importance of race obfuscates the ways in which germinal theoretical concepts reflect white, Eurocentric values while discriminating against other value systems. The following section explores the racial and ideological assumptions underpinning four widely accepted family therapy concepts.

Fusion and Differentiation. Concepts such as fusion and differentiation make assumptions about how much closeness and distance between family members constitute health and pathology. Unfortunately, minimal attention is devoted to considering how degrees of closeness and distance are culturally/racially relative. For instance, for many racial minorities, fusion may represent a culturally/racially sanctioned "way of being," and/or a healthy response to the psychological pressure imposed by racial oppression. It may serve an adaptive function that helps protect and insulate members against what is perceived as a threatening environment. Similarly, differentiation may represent alienation from a much needed, and/or greatly valued network of social-psychological support. Thus, for some families "we" (as they define it) may be more greatly valued than "I" (as Bowen defines it). Consequently, the manner in which these concepts implicitly reflect cultural/racial biases has remained unexamined.

Enmeshment and Disengagement. Two of the major concepts central to structural theory–"disengagement" and "enmeshment"–developed in vastly different racial/cultural contexts. Research and clinical work conducted with urban poor black and "Hispanic" families were instrumental in the conceptualization of disengagement. The concept of enmeshment, on the other hand, was shaped by the work done with middle income white families. Ironically, while these key concepts emerged from specific racial and cultural contexts, they have "generated a theory of therapy that has universal application" (Aponte & Van Deusen, 1981).

Recognizing the contexts out of which key structural theory concepts emerge helps to clarify their cultural relativity. For instance, for racial minorities, the closeness commonly associated with enmeshment often serves a functional role. Watson and Protinsky (1988) found that enmeshment is correlated positively with healthy ego identity development among black adolescents. Thus, when the concept of enmeshment is considered in relation to racial minority families, its universal meaning and the value ascribed to it must be approached with caution.

Developments in Theory. In recent years, increasingly, efforts have been made to contextualize family therapy by considering ways in which socio-cultural variables contribute to differences between families (MacKinnon & Miller, 1987). This philosophical shift is inspired in part by the Feminist Critique which challenges patriarchal assumptions embedded in family therapy theory and practice. The Feminist Critique led to the emergence of feminist informed family therapy which challenges the gender-biased constructions embedded in family therapy theory and practice (Goldner, 1985; Hare-Mustin, 1985; Taggart, 1985; Ault-Riché, 1986; Avis, 1986; Bograd, 1986; Goodrich, Rampage, Ellman, and Halstead, 1986; Walters, M., Carter, B., Papp, P., & Silverstein, O., 1988; McGoldrick, M., Anderson, C., & Walsh, F., 1989).

Highlighting this shift, other family therapy theorists also have begun to address the impact of the social context on family functioning. McGoldrick, Pearce, and Giordano (1982) discuss differences in family functioning among seventeen unique ethnic groups with strategies and recommendations for treatment. Imber-Black (1988) and Minuchin (1989) explore the ways in which families are impacted by larger systems. Mirkin (1990) analyzes the ways in which socio-cultural variables such as gender, poverty, and the threat of nuclear disaster impact families and the therapeutic process.

While each of these areas compensates for the historical lack of socio-cultural contexualization in family therapy, none effectively integrates issues of race. For instance, feminist informed family therapy fails to consider the ways in which gender issues differ among women depending on race and skin color. Many black women, and other women of color consistently maintain that racial issues are minimized by white feminists who see sexism as the dominant societal evil. The failure to address the complex relationship between race and gender greatly minimizes the utility of the feminist dialogue for some women of color.

McGoldrick et al. (1982) include chapters on racial minority groups (African Americans, Black West Indians, Puerto Ricans, etc.), however the issues are presented under the rubric of ethnicity with limited discussion of the impact of race and skin color. Similarly, the larger systems work of Imber-Black (1988) and Minuchin (1989) do not address racial issues specifically. Mirkin (1990) addresses race in a chapter on African American families but excludes a consistent analysis of how race impacts all families. Thus, despite efforts to contextualize family therapy socio-culturally, racial issues continue to be treated marginally.

Training Programs and Professional Organizations

Racial issues also receive minimal attention in training programs and professional organizations.

Training Programs. The ways in which racial issues are neglected in training programs has particularly profound implications for the field of family therapy. Training programs are the nest where future generations of family therapists are guided and nurtured. The knowledge, skills, and sensitivities they acquire (or do not acquire) impact their interactions with all clients. The messages programs communicate with regard to racial issues are critical.

Wilson and Stith (1993) explored the representation of African American students and faculty in marriage and family therapy training programs. A survey of 25 accredited MFT programs revealed that 3% of master's degree and 2.7% of doctoral degree students were African American. Less than 1% of the total number of master's degree and 1.8% of doctoral degree graduates were African American. Additionally, between 1989-1990, of 100 full-time and 50 part-time faculty, four of the full-time and two of the part-time positions were filled by African Americans. The relevance of this underrepresentation is reflected in concerns expressed by faculty and African American students regarding the efficacy of white students' clinical work with non-white clients.

Hardy and Laszloffy (1992) explore a variety of ways family therapy training programs overlook the importance of racial issues. One of the major ways in which this occurs is through inadequacies within curricular design. For instance, generic courses, particularly those addressing "cultural diversity," "ethnic minorities," or "multiculturalism," often unwittingly obscure race by over-focusing on less volatile issues such as ethnicity and culture. They also trivialize racial issues by segregating race-related content from the remainder of the curriculum.

The failure to recruit and retain racially diverse students and faculty is also cited as problematic. Programs comprised of student and faculty populations that are racially homogenous impart the message that it is not important to create contexts that encourage racial tolerance and exploration. The same is true for programs that have "only one" student or faculty present who differs racially from the remainder of the student and faculty populations. Essentially, the "only one" is bestowed unofficially with the responsibility of being the representative for "their group," as well as for all others who are "different."

Professional Organizations. Professional organizations exercise tremendous influence over the shape and direction of the field. The American Association for Marriage and Family Therapy (AAMFT) is one of two major professional associations representing the interests of marital and family therapy. The American Family Therapy Academy (AFTA) is the other national organization representing family therapy. While the professional goals of the two organizations differ quite substantially, there are some similarities. For example, both organizations are strongly committed to family well being, are located in Washington D.C., and have some overlap in membership. Another striking commonalty is the degree to which race is marginalized within, and by, each organization.

Racial marginalization within AAMFT and AFTA is reflected in their organizational structures, as well as in the content that is recognized and emphasized. Despite their long histories, neither organization reports a racial minority CEO or President of the Board of Directors. The professional staff of both organizations are either all or predominantly white. The AAMFT employs several non-white staff members, however they occupy a disproportionate number of the non-professional, non-administrative positions. Killian (in press) analyzed the annual AAMFT conference programs between 1980 and 1992 and found that the total percentage of programming devoted to minority issues was 5.28. The study also found that while there was a significant rise in the racial minority population within the last 13 years, there was no significant increase in the percentage of programming devoted to racial minority issues. Although comparable data for AFTA are not available, it is questionable whether the results would be dramatically different.

Clinical Practice

One of the major truisms in the field of psychotherapy is the assertion that potentially divisive societal issues such as race, gender, and a myriad of other socio-cultural variables become insignificant at the beginning of the clinical hour. This is especially true with regard to race, wherein therapists are encouraged to assume a neutral, colorblind stance. If overt acknowledgment or discussion of race related issues occurs, it is often considered an exception or distraction from more (legitimate) "intrapsychic" or "interpersonal/familial conflicts."

Race is always an organizing principle in therapy. Unfortunately, because of the marginalization process, therapists are often unprepared to recognize and/or respond to the relevance of race. Since the importance of race is often minimized, most therapists do not acquire the skills and sensitivities necessary to "see" and "talk" about the racial subtleties in therapy. The following section discusses several therapeutic obstacles which may arise when therapists are not prepared to deal with racial issues within therapy.

1. *The Impact of Marginalization on the Therapeutic Relationship.* The establishment of a trusting therapeutic relationship often requires therapists to validate the significance that race may hold for clients both within and outside of therapy. Frequently, the validation process involves identifying and acknowledging the ways in which clients may communicate about race. However, clients rarely communicate the significance that race holds for them directly. Rather, they tend to do so through the use of racial metaphors. Because of the marginalization of racial issues, most therapists are taught not to see or talk about race. Thus, identifying and/or responding effectively to racial metaphors is difficult. When therapists do not validate the ways in which clients communicate racially, they tend to "lose points," thereby undermining the establishment of trust in the therapeutic relationship. The following case highlights the presence of racial metaphors in therapy and how they organize the therapeutic system.

The Halloways

The Halloways, an interracial couple, had been experiencing marital difficulties which were characterized by continuous cycles of conflict and resolution. Their oldest son, Carlos, age 14, seemed to be the most affected by the confusing nature of his parents' relationship. He also expressed varying degrees of anger toward the therapist through his relentlessly challenging behavior. The therapist's first assumption was that the son's behavior represented "normal adolescent rebellion." While this hypothesis was certainly plausible, it did not address completely why virtually all of Carlos' verbal utterances consisted of covert racial comments. The parents, especially the father, also communicated with the therapist in a rather indirect and obtuse manner. In virtually every session the therapist was confronted with questions about some aspect of his personal life ranging from where he lived to what television programs he watched. Interestingly, he was never asked his views regarding interracial relationships. In fact, the topic of race was never introduced as a potential discussion point.

Carlos decided to break this pattern during the fourth session. He asked the therapist if he were "down with OPP." The therapist, who clearly did not understand the nature of the inquiry, ignored it. Carlos repeated the question several other times but the therapist avoided responding each time. While this pattern persisted, the parents smiled rather sheepishly admonishing their son that "he probably doesn't understand that type of language."

The term OPP is a colloquial expression extracted from a popular rap song bearing the same title. The expression is widely used by and among many urban African American teenagers. Of course, it is not unreasonable that the therapist would be unfamiliar with this expression, however, his failure to check out that which he may not have understood, impeded his ability to recognize that race was an issue for this boy, and maybe the entire family. The client was compelled to identify the racial disparities present in the room by challenging the therapist to also recognize and acknowledge these differences. While the son tested the therapist's racial sensitivity by wondering if he were "down with OPP," the parents conducted a slightly more sophisticated inquiry by seeking "significant" inferential information. Throughout all of this the therapist remained oblivious, and therefore failed to acknowledge the signals designed to affirm the significance of race.

While race was not related to this family's presenting problem, it constituted an important part of their realities. For whatever reasons however, the family preferred to communicate the significance of race through racial metaphors. Unfortunately, the therapist did not attend to these metaphorical expressions and hence, never validated the importance that race held for this family both outside of, as well as within therapy.

2. Therapist Generated Micro-Aggressions. The establishment of a trusting therapeutic relationship is contingent upon clients' perceptions regarding therapists' racial sensitivity. Due to the inattention devoted to racial issues within family therapy, therapists are not encouraged to explore themselves as racial beings. Most therapists are often unaware of their deeply held racial ideologies and the subtle ways in which such beliefs are expressed. This usually results in Therapist Generated Micro-aggressions (TGM) which are subtle, often unconscious acts of racial prejudice. Therapist Generated Micro-aggressions represent in one sense, "innocent" acts of racism that are unintentional in their expression and underlying hostility. However, the recipients of micro-aggressive acts often perceive them as offensive and hostile.

Therapist Generated Micro-aggressions undermine therapy because they reveal information about the therapist that may be incongruent with the more visible image projected. This clearly undermines trust. Although clients are almost always aware of the aggression, they have little recourse for addressing it directly. Due to the power differential, clients may not feel comfortable challenging the therapist with their perceptions of micro-aggressions. In cross-racial therapy, black clients, for example, are even less likely than white clients to point out therapist-generated micro-aggressions. Many blacks assume that their perceptions will be labeled as racial hypersensitivity or racial anger. The client's reticence to address the Therapist Generated Micro-aggressions directly, coupled with the therapist's inability to recognize them, create a major therapeutic impasse. The following vignette illustrates how a therapist's racial micro-aggression ultimately undermines the therapeutic relationship.

The Ahmeds

Dr. Elizabeth Manlove, a white family therapist with ten years clinical experience, sought consultation for a stuck case involving a black family, the Ahmeds. The identified patients were Jamar, 14, and Akbar, 12, who had been referred to Elizabeth by their mother Rashea. According to Ms. Ahmed, a single parent mother, her two sons constantly disobeyed her requests to not have their friends in the house when she was not at home. Ms. Ahmed worked from 11 a.m. to 7 p.m., and her sons were unsupervised between the time that school adjourned (approximately 2:30 p.m.) until she arrived home (approximately 7:45 p.m.). According to Ms. Ahmed, her next door neighbor had informed her that the boys typically had friends in the house from the time they arrived home from school to virtually minutes before she arrived home from work.

The therapist had two sessions with the family before they began to appear "resistant." She spent the first session gathering pertinent background data such as the childrens' ages, where they attended school, and Ms. Ahmed's place of employment. Akbar and Jamar were responsive to therapy and participated openly. The second session also appeared to progress smoothly. Dr. Manlove gathered more information as it related to the presenting problem. Specifically she explored with each family member their views with regard to such matters as Ms. Ahmed's work schedule, concerns around safety, the rules around having friends over, feelings about the boys' friends, their social needs and desires, etc. Overall, Dr. Manlove reported that second session, like the first, progressed moderately well.

During the third session Jamar refused to sit down. Elizabeth reported that she was extremely annoyed by his act of defiance. Although Jamar was participating in the therapy, he adamantly refused her numerous requests to sit down. After he refused what was announced as her final request, she stated: "listen, *we* don't stand in therapy . . . either you sit down or leave and come back when you're ready to sit." Jamar immediately left the room with his younger brother a few steps behind him. The family canceled the next session.

Although the therapist never intended any harm, her remark that "*we* don't stand in therapy" was experienced as a racial microaggression by the clients. The underlying motive(s) for Jamar's standing remain an enigma because the therapist, distracted by skin color, was unable to explore the motive(s) for his behavior. Dr. Manlove later acknowledged that Jamar's insistence on standing in the session was threatening: "he seemed so much bigger than me. . . . I guess I was uncomfortable with a large black male hovering over me." As the therapist's candor revealed, her comment was racially-driven and motivated by fear. This was apparent to the clients who terminated therapy shortly thereafter citing "cultural differences" as the reason, and requesting a referral to an African American therapist.

3. The Impact of Racial Marginalization on the Presenting Problem. Therapists are at risk of making one of two major types of assessment errors with regard to race. These are most likely to occur when therapists lack experience that fosters knowledge of and sensitivity to the subtleties of race. The two common assessment errors are Alpha and Beta.

Alpha Errors occur when a therapist assumes incorrectly that race is central to the presenting problem. Although at first glance it would appear that Alpha Errors are a function of hypersensitivity to race, in fact, it is the marginalization of race that is the catalyst for the misperception. Alpha Errors are committed typically because the therapist has not had sufficient exposure to different racial groups to make an effective (race related) differential diagnosis possible.

Beta Errors occur when race is central to the presenting problem, but is dismissed as unrelated. Lack of familiarity with racial issues often impedes the ability to recognize the subtle but pervasive ways in which race impacts the lives of clients in treatment. A Beta Error occurs when a therapist ignores or minimizes the impact of race or racism and focuses attention on finding the deeper psychological reason(s) for the problem.

Too Dark for Comfort

The therapist was a white male and the client was an interracial family. The family consisted of the mother, white; the father, black; and two biracial sons. The eldest son, age 12, was of a light complexion, while the youngest son, age 10, was dark complexioned. The family presented with the youngest son as the identified patient. The parents explained that over the past year their son had become increasingly withdrawn towards everyone except his mother and older brother, towards whom he had become increasingly hostile and aggressive. After attempting numerous solutions, the family, feeling overwhelmed and desperate, finally sought therapy.

After the initial session, the therapist consulted with the observing treatment team for nearly an hour. The entire discussion revolved around a variety of hypotheses and suggestions. Although the racial differences in the family were as overt as the divisions between family members, there was never any discussion of the issue of race. The silence around the racial differences continued to pervade the therapy throughout the following five sessions. Finally, during the sixth session, there was a breakthrough. The youngest son made an explosive confession by confronting his mother and telling her that the reason he hated her was because she had married his father. If she had not married him, then he would not have been born so dark! He proceeded to share in a rather painstaking manner how he felt plagued by being dark. He mentioned that his brother was more popular in school and at home because he was not dark. The son's confession was very painful for the entire family but it was a pivotal point in therapy. Initially, the therapist was verbally paralyzed by the son's disclosure. He made several unsuccessful attempts to persuade the son that perhaps there were other reasons for his anger. The son listened respectfully but remained adamant that he hated being dark and he resented his mother for it. During a post-session debriefing, the therapist remained unconvinced that race/skin color was integral to the son's acting out behavior.

Although race/skin color was an important dimension in this case, the family, the therapist and the treatment team, for whatever reasons, underestimated its relevance. As a result, the therapy's progress was unnecessarily slow.

As the previous case illustrations highlight, there are numerous ways in which the marginalization of racial issues can create therapeutic obstacles. Identifying and effectively managing the various ways race may or may not be related to therapy ultimately depends upon the therapist's understanding of and comfort with racial issues.

RECOMMENDATIONS AND FUTURE DIRECTIONS

Promoting racial inclusion in family therapy requires systemic change on multiple levels. Simplistic and uni-dimensional solutions such as adding racial minority content into training program curricula and recruiting people of color in professional organizations will have to be accompanied by more substantive changes. Namely, the field will have to experience an epistemological shift that will involve the re-examination of some of its most basic assumptions about the world and the people who comprise it. The following discussion briefly outlines a few salient recommendations that may serve as a catalyst for promoting this type of change.

Theory

Reliance on the Eurocentric ideology that permeates the field requires careful scrutiny and subsequent re-thinking. Virtually all universal truths with regard to family health and pathology, structure, and so forth necessitate renegotiation and ultimately reconceptualization. Shifting the field from a "universal" paradigm (Eurocentricism) to one that recognizes different truths represents a major challenge. To successfully execute such a task, the Eurocentricism that characterizes family therapy theory will have to be regarded for what it is—*one* of many possible truths rather than "the" truth. This potential shift has important implications with regard to a wide range of issues in family therapy that are related to "differences," especially racial issues. The recent emergence of two major movements, the postmodern and the multicultural movements, offers great potential in challenging the Eurocentricity that shapes family therapy theory.

Postmodernism. Postmodernism challenges the positivist notions of objective reality and absolute truth. It emphasizes the relativity of reality and the co-existence of multiple truths. From this perspective truth is viewed as something that is created, not discovered. Realities and truths are constructed through social interaction. Postmodernism advocates creating space for multiple voices to emerge so that each voice may define its experience–its reality. Postmodernism involves the recognition of multiple voices vying for multiple realities (Gergen, 1991). Operating from this premise, postmodernism within family therapy offers the potential for a shift toward a paradigm that supports the expression of multiple and varied worldviews. Thus, historically suppressed voices, such as those of racial minorities, women, and poor people will have the opportunity to emerge and define their realities. Furthermore, the universality of Eurocentricism will be challenged and recognized as "a" perspective rather than "the" perspective.

If postmodernism is to have a revolutionary impact on redesigning the existing paradigm in family therapy, it must move beyond intellectual discourse. Simply "dialoguing about differences" is insufficient. Rather a commitment to differences must be manifest in ways of living and being. In other words, it is imperative that persons have the opportunity to define their realities for themselves. This will require finding ways of living with the tension that often arises when different realities are able to co-exist. Relatedly, it is also important to challenge sophisticated attempts to equate "difference" with "inferior" and "dysfunctional." Challenging the tradition that equates "difference" with "inferiority" will necessitate integrating the concept of "power" into the dialogue–even if it is a social construction. Ignoring power and its relationship to race, gender, and class will serve as a painful reminder that "the more things change, the more they stay the same." If racial issues are to receive greater attention, it will be incumbent upon the proponents of postmodernism to resist the temptation of promoting and sterilizing differences simultaneously. If differences, in a generic sense, become the central focus of the dialogue, race and other socio-cultural constructions will remain marginalized.

Multiculturalism. The emphasis of the multicultural movement on exploring and appreciating cultural differences offers potential for greater recognition of racial significance. However, the inherent danger has been the tendency to couch highly charged racial issues in the less volatile language of multiculturalism. This phenomenon perpetuates the historic neglect of racial issues in favor of safer, more politically correct topics such as "ethnicity" and "cultural diversity."

The postmodern and the multicultural movements share in common a focus on the pluralistic ideal of recognizing and embracing differences. As these movements continue to permeate the field of family therapy it is increasingly likely that racial issues will receive more than cursory attention in family therapy. A commitment to pluralistic principles will lead inevitably to acknowledging race as a significant variable shaping the realities of all people in a particularly poignant way. The emergence of postmodernism and multiculturalism in family therapy challenges the epistemological foundation that governs the field. The very essence of these movements creates an opportunity to shift conceptually from the Eurocentric world-view of "homogeneity" to a worldview that promotes "pluralism."

Clinical Practice

To overcome the therapeutic obstacles which tend to arise as a function of the marginalization of race within the field, it is important that therapists discover ways to enhance their racial awareness and sensitivity. The following strategies are intended as a means of providing direction for challenging the marginalization of race outside of therapy. In this manner therapists will have opportunities to develop the skills and comfort that will enable them to recognize and respond more effectively to racial issues within therapy.

1. Enhance Cross-Racial Exposure. Enhancing cross racial exposure is a critical tool for developing comfort with cross racial interactions. Meaningful cross racial exposure can be obtained through a variety of experiences. Attending a religious service of another racial group, or participating in social, recreational, or political activities sponsored by different racial groups provide important cross-racial exposure.

Participation in meaningful cross racial experiences is imperative for all therapists. This is especially true for white therapists who may spend much of their personal lives isolated from significant contact with racial minorities. Cross racial exposure allows therapists to discover emotions and beliefs that have been suppressed or unexplored within themselves. It promotes the type of self-exploration that is central to becoming a racially sensitive therapist.

2. Challenge Colorblindness and Silence with Regard to Race. When therapists begin exposing themselves to different racial experiences they are challenging themselves to "see" race and skin color. This often leads to greater awareness of the numerous ways in which race and skin color organize common everyday experiences. For instance, therapists may begin to notice such things as the racial configurations of "couples on the street," correlations between race/skin color and the types of jobs people fill, and how different races are represented in the media. With regard to therapy, therapists will likely become more attuned to the racial identities of therapists, trainers, supervisors, administrators, clerical assistants, and clients; how race is addressed on intake forms, if at all; how race influences case referrals and assignments; and what types of racial messages–implicit or explicit–are transmitted through the clinical milieu (e.g., office artwork, magazines, music, etc.).

Eventually, as therapists grow increasingly attuned to racial issues, and increase their exposure to cross-racial situations, they will gradually acquire the courage to risk engaging in race-related (especially cross-racial) dialogues. These dialogues may initially involve low-intensity subjects, such as the importance of diversity. Even low intensity racially-based discussions can help to clarify one's racial ideology, challenge racial assumptions and stereotypes, and increase comfort with addressing racial issues directly. As personal comfort with race-related discussions increases, these dialogues may begin to focus on more intense issues, such as racism and personal prejudice. It is crucial therapists begin to "practice" talking about race, particularly with each other. Once they acquire the experience of talking candidly and comfortably about racial issues outside of therapy, it facilitates responsiveness to racial issues in therapy.

The following vignettes provide illustrations of how two therapists, who have engaged in racial self-exploration, effectively avoided the pitfalls that tend to arise as a result of the marginalization of race within family therapy.

Jabree and the T-Shirt

Jabree was a 15-year-old middle income African American adolescent. He was referred to a white female therapist, by his parents' African American therapist. In the first session Jabree made it clear that he was not happy to be there. It was difficult to discern how much of his behavior was attributable to adolescence, and how much, if any, was a function of the cross racial nature of the therapeutic system. The first session was characterized initially by long periods of silence. The dialogue between the therapist and the client was sparse. Although numerous attempts were made to engage the client in a dialogue, he merely shrugged his shoulders and often stated "I don't know."

After periods of protracted silence, the client finally began talking, but using colloquial expressions almost exclusively. "When I get out of school I'm usually down with my posse," he noted during one session. The therapist attempted to join with the client by adopting the use of some of his expressions. However, she selected only the ones with which she was familiar and asked him for explanations of terms she did not understand. He appeared to derive great delight in using expressions that the therapist did not understand fully. Despite her lack of understanding, the therapist remained respectful, quizzical, and composed.

Midway through the session, the therapist acknowledged a T-shirt the client was wearing with a picture of Africa and several prominent African-Americans on it. She commented that she recognized some of the faces, however she was somewhat embarrassed because as a white person there were many that she did not know. She asked for his help in identifying the prominent historical characters. The conversation about the "shirt" appeared to alter the therapeutic climate. By the end of the session, the client and the therapist were engaged in a mutually animated conversation. The difference in affect from start to finish was striking.

As it turned out, race was not a critical dimension of the presenting problem in this case. But it was a critical dimension of the therapeutic system. The therapist's ability to recognize and respectfully acknowledge the racial differences and the client's unique racial/cultural identity helped facilitate trust and joining. The therapist in this case had devoted a great deal of time to exploring herself as a racial being. An integral part of her exploration involved frequent racially-based dialogues with therapists of varied racial backgrounds. She also spent a great deal of time interacting socially with African Americans. As a result she was attuned to herself as a racial being and had the necessary awareness and comfort to recognize and respectfully validate the racial dimensions of the therapeutic system.

The Long Ride Home

The therapist was a white female and the client was a white family comprised of the mother, Ann; and two daughters, Jane, age 16; and Sally, age 13. The family had sought therapy because Ann and Jane were concerned with what seemed to be Sally's excessive moodiness and irritability. Sally reported during the first few sessions that no one in the family had time anymore to help with her homework or to "just hang out." This was a surprise to Ann and Jane who felt that it was Sally who did not want to spend time with them. After Sally's disclosure, Jane acknowledged that she had been absorbed with her new friends and perhaps she was not as attentive as she used to be toward her sister. Ann also confessed that her busy schedule had made her less available to Sally than in the past. She recently began working full-time and while she loved her new job she often felt tired. Thus, the focus of therapy shifted from Sally's moodiness to the changes that the family was undergoing as each person adapted to new roles.

During the beginning of the fourth session Ann began with her typical description of how her day had been quite exhausting. She added that today even the bus ride home had been long and stressful because "this black man sitting next to me was smoking cigarettes non-stop." The therapist was quizzical about the racial/gender qualification. She thought it was significant that Ann noted that the person sitting next to her was "male" and "black." She sensed that Ann's stress and aggravation had been exacerbated by the smoker's racial/gender identity. Thus she responded by asking: "what significance does it hold for you that the smoker was a black man?" Ann seemed stunned temporarily and then proceeded to assure the therapist it was not significant.

At that moment, the therapist noticed Jane roll her eyes. The therapist commented on this although Jane denied having done so. However, when Ann confirmed that she also had observed Jane's reaction, she finally retorted, "I guess I think it was significant to you that the man was black." When prompted further by the therapist, Jane explained that she thought her mother did not like black people very much. Ann appeared shocked, but other than denying the allegation, said nothing. The therapist asked Jane why she felt this way and she explained that when she was 12 she had a friend come over who was black. She said she will never forget that her mother treated her friend in a noticeably less cordial way than she treated her other (white) friends. For this reason, Jane said that from that time on she avoided introducing any of her black friends to her mom. What ensued from that point was a candid discussion between the family members regarding race. Eventually this led to Jane's disclosing that she had dated cross-racially although she had been afraid to tell her mother.

While Ann was hurt by Jane's secrecy, together they were able to discuss what this meant in their relationship, and come to a point of mutual understanding concerning their respective thoughts and feelings with regard to racial issues.

The therapist in this case was attuned to racial issues in therapy which enabled her to identify and comment on the mother's seemingly benign reference to race. In so doing, the therapist was demonstrating racial awareness and sensitivity. By commenting on the racial reference, the therapist was inviting the clients to contemplate their racial ideologies. While this may not always result in the emergence of a larger issue as it did in this case, it is one way to challenge the marginalization of race in therapy.

Training

Clinical training programs, both structurally and epistemologically, are the major perpetrators of racial marginalization. We have cited the numerous ways in which training programs unwittingly promote the marginalization of minority related issues both in terms of program culture and structure (Hardy, 1991; Hardy and Laszloffy, 1992). The following represents an illustrative list of strategies that might be employed to enhance the recognition of race in family therapy training.

1. Become Conversant with the Culture of the Program. Training programs like all other organized systems have rules, values, and mores that govern the behavior and participation of its membership. The first critical step in preparing racially/culturally competent therapists is to recognize and identify the cultural norms of the program with regard to race. Faculty and student composition, the collective values of student and faculty, teaching methodologies, and program design are some of the salient factors that contribute to the shaping of the program culture. The program culture is so endemic to the program that its many ramifications may not be readily discernible to those entrenched in it. Since this component of the program is usually the net result of implicitly negotiated rules, it is often necessary to utilize the services of an outside consultant to facilitate the identification of the culture.

2. Diversify Teaching Strategies. A critical analysis of the teaching strategies utilized by the program is the next step toward incorporating race and preparing racially/culturally competent therapists. The dominant mode of teaching in most training programs is based on Eurocentric principles. Consequently, a high premium is placed on abstract thinking, verbal expression, individual competition, and hierarchical classification. Teaching styles that favor Eurocentric principles also favor students whose worldviews have been shaped similarly. Anderson (1988) noted that the pervasiveness of Eurocentric modes of teaching force non-white students to be "bicultural, bidialectic, and bicognitive," while simultaneously punishing them for expressions or ways of learning that are non-Eurocentric.

To promote racial diversity and sensitivity, family therapy training programs must adopt teaching strategies that embrace principles of non-Western, non-Eurocentric perspectives. Styles of teaching that promote group cooperation, affective and experiential methods, and holistic and concrete thinking play an instrumental role in diversifying the modes of instruction within a training program. Diverse modes of teaching also acknowledge that students learn differently. It prevents the unintended consequences of punishing racial minority students whose dominant styles of learning may not be based on Eurocentric principles. Moreover, it also challenges white students to grapple with issues of biculturality and biraciality.

3. Integrate Curriculum. Successfully incorporating race into the entirety of the clinical training will require the program to integrate discussions about race in all courses throughout the curriculum. Creating a separate course to address race while simultaneously excluding the topic from other areas of the curriculum only reinforces the marginalization of race. The infusion of racial dimensions throughout the curriculum acknowledges the centrality of race with regard to all aspects of family life and family therapy. It encourages students to habitually challenge claims of color-blindness. In fact, this approach to the curriculum design encourages students to see color, and develop comfort discussing it.

4. Recruitment and Retention of Racially Diverse Students and Faculty. One of the most effective vehicles for accelerating a program's implementation of the aforementioned strategies is to recruit and retain racially diverse students and faculty. If the milieu of the program is one of openness and sensitivity to differences, racially diverse students and faculty can create a healthy tension in the program that enhances racial awareness and sensitivity. The program, however, must act counter-intuitively to resist the urge to reshape racial minorities into non-racial minority clones. Reshaping is likely to occur when students and faculty are "coerced into suppressing their racial identities and idiosyncrasies so that they will fit comfortably into the system" (Hardy & Laszloffy, 1992).

5. Conduct Racially-Focused Self of the Therapists' Work. Although most family therapy training programs emphasize the importance of self of the therapist work, it is rare that more than cursory attention is devoted to an examination of racial and cultural issues as they relate to the therapist. Race is a core dimension of the identity of racial minorities. It is an important means of defining oneself. The many manifestations of society's sensitivity to skin color serves as a constant reminder to people of color that they are different. Whites, on the other hand, only experience their racial selves when interacting as a numerical minority with people of color. Thus they are not challenged constantly to think of themselves racially. The use of structured exercises to critically examine racial components of the therapist's self can be quite effective in promoting racial awareness and sensitivity.

These exercises can be instrumental in achieving the following goals: (a) reconstructing the concept of race from a term that is considered synonymous with black, to one that includes black, white, brown, and yellow; (b) promoting the significance of race as it relates to one's self which is a prerequisite to understanding the importance it may have for others; (c) and demystifying race by encouraging open discussions and opportunities for healthy cross-racial tensions.

THE SIGNIFICANCE OF RACE, SELF, AND AN ETHICAL IMPERATIVE

Therapists dedicated to challenging the marginalization of racial issues in the field accept the ethical imperative that change begins with "self," not "other." Often times it is assumed that it is "other," rather than "self" who must change. This assumption impairs the possibility for growth and change because ultimately persons can only change "self," not "other." The act of exploring one's "self" is akin to a "looking within" process.

The "looking within" process requires therapists to explore their racial identities and beliefs, and to challenge the ways in which their roles as therapists are impacted. While many therapists believe, for example, that they can separate their everyday lives from their roles as therapists, this is virtually impossible. What occurs outside of therapy impacts what happens in therapy. For instance, can therapists really appreciate the humor in "an innocent racial joke" without having their racial sensitivity tempered? "Can therapists make references to niggers, spics, and white trash and then treat African Americans, Puerto Ricans, and whites respectfully and effectively in therapy?" (Hardy, 1993). Or, can therapists really expect that they can live their lives personally segregated from the everyday experiences of members of "other" races and provide effective therapy to these "others"? Is it possible to live in one of the most color conscious societies in the world and denounce race/skin color as a major organizing principle in therapy? It is imperative for therapists to explore the ways in which their "selves" prevent the establishment of meaningful relationships with "others," even when it is the "others" who are perceived to be different.

NOTES

1. Any reference throughout the paper to people of color should be construed as all inclusive. References to blacks or African Americans (interchangeable terms) are used only when there is a notable distinction to be made between this group and people of color.

2. The term race will be used in this paper with the understanding that skin color is a phenomenon that is both a part of and distinct from race. The term skin color will only be used when the distinction is critical.

3. The term race will be used in this paper both denotatively and connotatively.

REFERENCES

Anderson, J. A. (1988). Cognitive styles and multicultural populations. *Journal of Teacher Education*, pp. 5-6.

Aponte, H. (1974). Psychotherapy for the poor: An eco-structural approach to treatment. *Delaware Medical Journal, 46*, 432-448.

Aponte, H. (1976). Underorganization in the poor family. In P. J. Guerin (Ed.), *Family Therapy: Theory and Practice*. New York: Gardner Press.

Aponte, H., & Van Deusen, J. (1981). Structural Family Therapy. In A. S. Gurman & D. P. Kniskern, (Eds.), *Handbook of Family Therapy, Volume I*. New York: Brunner/Mazel.

Ault-Riché, M. (1986). *Women and Family Therapy*. Rockville, MD: Aspen.

Avis, J. (1986). Feminist issues in family therapy. In F. Piercy & D. Sprenkle (Eds.), *Family Therapy Sourcebook*. New York: Guilford Press.

Bagarrozi, D. (1980). Family therapy and the black middle class: A neglected area of study. *Journal of Marital and Family Therapy, 6*, 159-166.

Bograd, M. (1986). A feminist examination of family therapy: What is a woman's place? In D. Howard (Ed.), *The Dynamics of Feminist Therapy*. New York: The Haworth Press, Inc.

Bograd, M. (1987). Enmeshment, fusion or relatedness?: A conceptual analysis. *Journal of Psychotherapy and the Family*, 3, 65-80.

Boyd-Franklin, N. (1989). *Black Families in Therapy: A Multisystems Approach*. New York: Guilford.

Elzur, J., & Minuchin, S. (1989). *Institutionalizing Madness*. New York: Basic Books.

Gergen, K. J. (1991). *The Saturated Self: Dilemnas of Identity in Contemporary Life*. New York: Basic Books.

Goldner, V. (1985). Feminism in family therapy. *Family Process*, 24, 31-47.

Goodrich, T., Rampage, C., Ellman, B., & Halstead, K. (1988). *Feminist Family Therapy: A Casebook*. New York: W. W. Norton.

Hardy, K. V. (1991). The theoretical myth of sameness: A critical issue in family therapy training and treatment. In G. W. Saba, B. M. Karrer, & K. V. Hardy (Eds.), *Minorities and Family Therapy*. New York: The Haworth Press, Inc.

Hardy, K. V., & Laszloffy, T. A. (1992). Training racially sensitive family therapists: Context, content, and contact: *Families in Society*, 73(6), 364-370.

Hardy, K. V. (1993). War of the worlds. *Family Therapy Networker*, July-August, 50-57.

Hare-Mustin, R. (1987). The problems of gender in family therapy. *Family Process*, 26, 15-27.

Hines, P. (1988). The family life cycle of poor black families. In B. Carter & M. McGoldrick (Eds.), *The Changing Family Life Cycle* (2nd. ed.). New York: Gardner Press.

Imber-Black, E. (1988). *Families and Larger Systems: A Therapist's Guide Through the Labyrinth*. New York: Guilford.

James, K., & McIntyre, D. (1983). The reproduction of families: The social role of family therapy? *Journal of Marital and Family Therapy*, 9, 119-129.

Killian, K. D. (In press). *Minority Representation in Family Therapy: A Study of AAMFT Conference Program Content and Members' Perceptions*.

MacKinnon, L., & Miller, D. (1987). The new epistemology and the Milan approach: Feminist and sociopolitical considerations. *Journal of Marital and Family Therapy*, 13, 139-155.

McGoldrick, M., Pearce, J., & Giordano, J. (Eds.). (1982). *Ethnicity and Family Therapy*. New York: Guilford.

McGoldrick, M., Anderson, C., & Walsh, F. (1989). *Women in Families: A Framework for Family Therapy*, New York: Norton.

Minuchin, S., & Montalvo, B. (1966). An approach for diagnosis of the low socioeconomic family. *American Psychiatric Research Report*, 20.

Minuchin, S., & Montalvo, B. (1967). Techniques for working with disorganized low socio-economic families. *American Journal of Orthopsychiatry*, 37, 380-387.

Mirkin, M. P. (1990). *The Social and Political Contexts of Therapy*. Needham Heights, Maine: Allyn & Bacon.

Morris, J. R. (1987). Family-of-origin and family therapy considerations with black families. In J. C. Hansen, *Family of Origin*, Aspen: Rockville, Maryland.

Nobles, W. W. (1978). Toward an empirical and theoretical framework for defining black families. *Journal of Marriage and the Family,* 40(4), 679-688.

Taggart, M. (1985). The feminist critique in epistemological perspective: Questions of context in family therapy. *Journal of Marital and Family Therapy,* 11, 113-126.

Walters, M., Carter, B., Papp, P., & Silverstein, O. (1988). *The Invisible Web.* New York: Guilford.

Watson, M. F., & Protinsky, H. D. (1988). Black adolescent identity development: Effects of perceived family structure. *Family Relations,* 37(3), 288-292.

Wheeler, D., Avis, J., Miller, L., & Chaney, S. (1986). Rethinking family therapy education and supervision: A feminist model. *Journal of Psychotherapy and the Family,* 1, 53-71.

Wilson, L. L., & Stith, S. M. (1993). The voices of African American MFT students: Suggestion for improving recruitment and retention. *Journal of Marital and Family Therapy,* 19(1), 17-30.

LatiNegra:
Mental Health Issues
of African Latinas

Lillian Comas-Díaz

SUMMARY. The LatiNegra, the daughter of African American and Latino parents, is presented. Her racial and gender exclusions throughout her life cycle are discussed, in addition to their impact on her mental health status. Family and collective dynamics surrounding the LatiNegras' experiences include intense ambivalence, conflict, shame, guilt, projection, plus racial and gender stereotyping. As the victim of racism and sexism, in addition to *racismo* and *sexismo*, the LatiNegra frequently suffers from a fragmented identity and conflict within her loyalties and needs for acceptance and belonging. Consequently, two of the LatiNegra's major mental health issues are low self-esteem and exposure to multiple trauma. Empowerment and feminist family therapy approaches are presented as being relevant to the LatiNegra's mental health needs.

INTRODUCTION: YOU DON'T LOOK LATINA!

This assertion is a continual reminder to the LatiNegra that a significant portion of her culture and ethnicity is forcefully denied.

Lillian Comas-Díaz, PhD, is affiliated with Transcultural Mental Health Institute, 1301 20th NW, Suite 711, Washington, DC 20036.

The author would like to thank Rhea Almeida for her insightful editorial suggestions; Janice Petrovich, Angela Ginorio, Sandra Laureano, and Mercedes del Valle Rana for their contributions; and María Providencia Scott for her inspirational influence.

[Haworth co-indexing entry note]: "LatiNegra: Mental Health Issues of African Latinas." Comas-Díaz, Lillian. Co-published simultaneously in the *Journal of Feminist Family Therapy* (The Haworth Press, Inc.) Vol. 5, No. 3/4, 1994, pp. 35-74; and: *Expansions of Feminist Family Theory Through Diversity* (ed: Rhea V. Almeida) The Haworth Press, Inc., 1994, pp. 35-74. Multiple copies of this article/chapter may be purchased from The Haworth Document Delivery Center [1-800-3-HAWORTH; 9:00 a.m. - 5:00 p.m. (EST)].

35

The LatiNegra is the African Latina who is perceived beyond any doubt as Black by both the North American and the Latino communities. The LatiNegra is the daughter of African American (Caribbean, North, Central and South American) and Latino parents. Although there are some differences between the African North American LatiNegra and the African Caribbean LatiNegra, the racial exclusions faced by both LatiNegras embrace many commonalities. For instance, the denial of LatiNegras' Latinness is equally emphasized by all communities. Consequently, the LatiNegra constitutes a classic example of racial exclusion, marginality, and disconnection. Frequently, her combination of race, ethnicity, and gender result in her being a minority within a minority.

This article addresses racial and life cycle exclusions of LatiNegras and their impact on the mental health of these women. Due to the heterogeneity among these populations, I will concentrate on LatiNegras with a Caribbean background. I emphasize themes prevalent among multiracial women, such as acceptance and belonging, sexuality, and identity (Root, in press), which have also been identified as prevalent among LatiNegras (del Valle, personal communication, 1993). Family and collective dynamics surrounding the LatiNegras' unique experiences often include intense ambivalence, racial projection, conflict in ethno-racial loyalty, shame, racial and gender stereotyping, and guilt. Feminist and family therapy approaches will be discussed and vignettes will be used to illustrate particular points. Clinical data have been altered to protect confidentiality.

HISTORICAL AND SOCIOPOLITICAL CONTEXT

The Latino/Hispanic population comprises a rich tapestry of races and ethnicities including but not limited to American Indians, Africans, Spaniards and other Europeans. The presence of the African heritage varies among the diverse Latin American countries. For instance, Brazil, Columbia, Cuba, the Dominican Republic, Ecuador, Panama, Puerto Rico, and Venezuela have significant Black African populations, while countries such as Uruguay, Chile, and particularly, Argentina have virtually no Blacks due to racial genocide. Black individuals from West Africa were sold as slaves in the Spanish Caribbean to work in sugar cane plantations. Consequently, the population with African ancestry is highly visible in the Caribbean, particularly in Cuba, Puerto Rico, and the Dominican Republic. Moreover, Cuban, Dominican, and Puerto Rican LatiNegras often share historical, cultural, and geopolitical commonalities.

Racial Glossary

In discussing the issues affecting the LatiNegra, I need to define my terms. I use the term *LatiNegra* as opposed to *Africana Latina,* in order to avoid the partial or total negation of the Latinness in African Latinas by the Latino community. Within the Spanish linguistic usage, the first word–Latina–is the primary denomination, while the second word–Negra–is the secondary denomination or adjective. African Latinos have objected to the Spanish use of the terms *Africano Latino* or *Negro Latino* because this semantic usage reflects the racism of denying the Latinness of African Latinos (Zenón Cruz, 1975). The term *LatiNegra* attempts to recognize both ethnicity and race, while resisting the society's systematic negation of African Latinas' Latinness. This systematic negation is the product of racism. In a culture that values interconnectedness, the external forces of racism are so powerful that they result in oppressing and separating Latinos through color lines. Consequently, the term *LatiNegra* is an empowering affirmation of both the Latino and African components of the African Latina's multi ethno-racial identity.

Racial differences among Caribbean Latinos are expressed according to gradations of color and features. For example, *mulata* is the equivalent of female mulatto; *jabá* is the light-skinned woman who has features that indicate Black ancestry–equivalent to the African American yellow; *grifa* is the female with White features that has frizzled or kinky hair; *trigueña* is the female who is olive skinned; *morena* is darker than the *trigueña, india* has Indian characteristics, and *negra* or *prieta* is the Black female (Comas-Díaz, 1989, Jorge, 1979; Longres, 1974).

Relationships between individuals with different racial appellations are mediated by historical, political, social, and economic factors. During slavery, lighter skinned Blacks (presumedly the progeny of White plantation owners) were preferred over darker skinned slaves as house servants. Although this preferred treatment did not shelter them from slavery or abuse, the difference in treatment affected the relationships between lighter and darker slaves, creating jealousies and resentments (Greene, 1992). The legacy of North American preferential treatment based on skin color resulted in many Black and White persons' developing skin color preferences, feelings, resentments, and distortions about such preferences (Greene, 1992). This legacy is also present in the Caribbean.

Racismo: Latino Style Racism

Many Caribbean Latinos describe their racial background as a rainbow, acknowledging their mixed Indian, Spaniard and African heritage. Contrary to the North American dictum that one drop of African blood makes you Black, one drop of White blood makes you at least not Black in the Latin Caribbean (Longres, 1974). The historical recognition of the rainbow racial composition of the Spanish Caribbean was partly the outcome of the Catholic religion. Although the church officially discouraged intermarriage, its condemnation of sexual cohabitation as *living in sin*, facilitated the legalization of interracial unions. Additionally, common-law marriages have a history of being more legally recognized in the Latino society than in North American society. Therefore, the offspring of such unions were often recognized by the society.

The Spanish Caribbean history of relative miscegenation allows the individual to recognize his or her African ancestry. For instance, Puerto Ricans who look White cannot deny their African heritage. The saying, *Y tu abuela dónde está?* (And where is your grandmother?), illustrates that Puerto Ricans have a female ancestor (i.e., grandmother, great-grandmother) who was Black African and thus, they cannot deny their own blackness regardless of phenotype or how non-Black they appear to be. The emphasis on the femaleness of the Black ancestor derives from the collective memory of dark females being sexually enslaved and raped by *conquistadores* or other White Europeans. This emphasis acknowledges the intersecting influence of misogyny and slavery. However, racism among Latinos is very much alive, regardless of the visibility of the African Caribbean *abuelas*.

Racismo or Latino style racism, permeates all spheres of the society from education, politics, religion, arts, and business; to social, personal, family, sexual, and interpersonal relationships (Zenón Cruz, 1975). *Racismo* is a classic example of internalized racism. For example, many Caribbean Latinos have difficulties accepting their own blackness and often accuse each other of being Black and/ or having African ancestry (racial projection). The reply *el que not tiene dinga tiene mandinga* (the individual who does not have *dinga* has *mandinga*) asserts that Latinos who don't have *dinga* (Indian heritage) have *mandinga* (African heritage) (Zenón Cruz, 1975). Many times this reply is used to combat racist remarks, racial projection, and covert *racismo*.

Internalized racism is pervasive in the Latin Caribbean media. The media often portray the idealized image of Caribbean Latinos as being non-Black. The Puerto Rican movie, *Lo que le pasó a Santiago* (What happened to Santiago), nominated for the 1990 foreign movie Oscar, did not have Black, *jabao*, or *grifo* actors. This behavior can be interpreted as an attempt at passing, or Latino Caribbeans' effort to appear as non-Blacks. Passing involves a racial denial and active attempts to be perceived (by self and others) as White, or at least, non-Black. Greene (1992) has argued that among African Americans, passing has been used historically as an adaptive survival mechanism because it has enabled its users to avoid imminent harm or to obtain goods, services or jobs that would be otherwise denied because of discrimination. However, she also warns us that when passing is accompanied by the belief that being Black is a sign of inferiority, it represents an expression of internalized racism. Similarly, the darkest actor in the *Lo que le pasó a Santiago* film–a dark Indian looking *trigueño*–played the role of a criminal. This *casting* subliminally designates criminals as being non-White individuals.

Compared to North American racism, *racismo* appears as a different construct. *Racismo* is a dynamic, fluid, and contextual concept which is often associated with social class. Regardless of color, the higher the person's social class, the whiter the person is perceived to be, and thus, less subjected to *racismo*. Therefore, you can change your color when you change your socioeconomic class. Thus, *racismo* is highly contextualized but it is not as institutionalized as North American racism. Due to the specific historic-political context and the relativity of color and racial attributions, many

Latinos pride themselves in being non-racist. This assertion is at best a distortion and/or denial, and at worst a racist act. Zenón Cruz (1975) asserts that a mechanism of covert *racismo* among Caribbean Latinos is racial projection. He argues that when asked directly about *racismo* many Latinos may not identify themselves as racist, while they identify their neighbors, friends, even relatives, as being racist, thus, attributing to others their own *racismo*.

Racismo tends to operate differently from racism. It appears to be relatively covert compared to racism because the Latino Caribbean society is historically more racially integrated than the North American one. The covert nature of *racismo* among Caribbean Latinos acquires complex connotations, due to both its societal and individual dimensions. An example of an individual dimension is racial perception. Both racial perception and identification comprise subjective and highly complex processes. Racial perception of others is also related to the individuals' self racial perception. As an illustration, Ginorio (1971) empirically examined racial perception in Puerto Rico, and found that individuals' perceptions were closely associated to their own racial identification. In other words, a *trigueña* may be racially perceived differently by two individuals according to their individual self racial identification. The same *trigueña* may be perceived as being darker by a darker observer, and lighter by a lighter observer. Del Valle (1989) replicated Ginorio's study in the United States, obtaining similar findings.

Though different, *racismo* is as painful, dysfunctional, and destructive as its North American counterpart. The combination of racism, sexism, and classism contributes to the covert nature of racismo and this covert nature, further involves the rejection of LatiNegras. It has been shown that there is a sociocultural glass ceiling for the LatiNegros in general, and for the LatiNegra in particular (Ramos Rosado, 1986). Although Latinos may not object to socializing with LatiNegros, they profoundly object to their offsprings' decision to marry LatiNegros. Particularly, having a LatiNegra daughter-in-law, as opposed to a LatiNegro son-in-law, is often perceived as the decline of the family's status and class. As an illustration, it is usually more acceptable for a female to marry down by marrying a LatiNegro, than for a male to marry down by marrying a LatiNegra. Due to their gender, LatiNegros often have more options for marriage–LatiNegras, Latinas, Whites, and African American females. If the LatiNegro marries a non-Black female, such liaison is less threatening than a LatiNegra marrying a non-Black man.

Marrying a LatiNegra is contrary to the Latino dictum of *adelantar o mejorar la raza* (literally, to improve the race)–going through a whitening process by marrying someone light skinned or White (Jorge, 1979). Therefore, LatiNegras are not perceived as desirable potential spouses because they do not *improve the race,* instead, they *damage the race* (Zenón Cruz, 1975). This process is compounded by the fear of *requintar* (from the word *fifth*), or the inheritance of African traits not manifested in the parents or grandparents but present in a fifth generation (great-grandparent) ancestor. Thus, non-Black Latinos fear that their African ancestry has greater probability of *requintar* in their children, grandchildren, or great grandchildren if they marry LatiNegros or non-White Latinos. The fear of *requintar* may acquire obsessive proportions in that individuals engage in excruciating racial denial and projection. These dynamics are perpetuated in an elitist, racist, sexist, and patriarchal system.

The primary role of the mother in the socialization process among Latinos also contributes to the rejection of LatiNegras as potential wives. LatiNegras are considered more threatening to the family racial character (even to the national racial character) than LatiNegro fathers. Because Latina mothers are expected to be physically and emotionally present in the lives of their offspring, while such expectation does not necessarily apply to fathers, who occasionally, are allowed to be emotionally and physically distant. Consequently, LatiNegro fathers are less visible than LatiNegra mothers, while the presence of the LatiNegra mother is harder to hide in the family racial closet than the LatiNegro father. A visible LatiNegra mother is a clear sign of her children's mixed racial ancestry, reducing their opportunities to *adelantar la raza* (improve the race), and thus, limiting their attractiveness as potential spouses.

Marrying a LatiNegra may additionally tap into internalized racism and misogyny, due to the racial and gender connotations attributed to LatiNegras. These processes are facilitated by the special racial and gender projection that LatiNegras may engender in a patriarchal and covertly racist society. I expand more on these issues in the section on racial and gender dynamics.

The realities of LatiNegras are compounded by the interaction of gender, race, class, and sexual orientation. LatiNegras' circumstances are very different than those of other Latinas. The unique realities of the Caribbean LatiNegra are beginning to be acknowledged. For example, the Puerto Rican Government Office of Women's Issues sponsored a 1992 conference on the Black Puerto Rican woman (de Guzman, personal communication, 1993). Another example of this recognition is the formation of LatiNegras' organizations such as the *Unión de Mujeres Puertorriqueñas Negras* (Union of Black Puerto Rican Women) (Petrovich, personal communication, 1993). Unfortunately, the issues of the LatiNegra in the United States have received minimal attention (Jorge, 1979).

COLLECTIVE CONTEXTS: FAMILY AND COMMUNITY

Latinos in the United States are identified as both ethnic and racial minorities. Many Latinos' racial experiences in the United States surpass the individual and family and need to be viewed as a collective experience where all are forced to confront and question their racial identity. The individual and institutionalized racism prevalent in the United States encourages a racial division among Caribbean Latinos. Most of them are multiracial individuals and while living in the continental United States, frequently internalize North American racism. Mainstream society, with its polarized racial identification, often forces Latinos with African heritage into defining themselves as either Black or White.

LatiNegras' needs for acceptance and belonging to their families and communities are plagued by conflict. Traditionally, the family acts as a buffer between a child and her outside world. However, the Latino family does not buffer the LatiNegra against racism nor *racismo*. Bearing different gradations of color, family members may be inept to cope with the North American racism. One or both of the LatiNegra's parents may not be considered African Latinos and cannot teach her the coping mechanisms to deal with racial prejudice and discrimination as a Black woman. They are unable to racially socialize their LatiNegra daughter. Racial socialization involves warning Black girls about the racial dangers and disappointments without overwhelming or overprotecting them (Greene, 1990). Although the LatiNegra's parents may be able to effectively teach her how to cope with ethnic discrimination and prejudice as a Latina, they cannot empower her by teaching her emotional defenses and coping skills as a Black female. Racial and gender socialization is further complicated by the great differences between the non-LatiNegra mother's racial experiences and those of her LatiNegra daughter.

The LatiNegra who is a lesbian is even more severely affected relative to her needs for acceptance and belonging. Besides the mainstream society's racism, sexism, and heterosexism, many lesbians of color face the additional stress of coping with the gay and lesbian community's racism, plus the heterosexism, sexism and internalized racism of their own ethnic community (Greene, 1993; Kanuha, 1990). This situation creates profound conflicts in the lesbian LatiNegra's loyalties in addition to paradoxes within her identity and sense of belonging. For instance, Kanuha (1990) argues that for many lesbians of color the contradiction in feeling safe yet afraid as lesbians in their ethnic communities is evidence of the pervasiveness of both racism and sexism. She recognizes a critical tie between homophobia and sexism, where many people of color identify lesbianism as a White phenomenon, thus, blaming the existence of lesbians of color on White feminism. The outcome of this process is that the lesbian LatiNegra is further excluded from all the communities to which she attempts to belong.

The Latino family's lack of racial socialization and racial coping skills affects the LatiNegra differently than the LatiNegro because culturally, females tend to derive self-esteem from receiving approval from significant others. In the general culture, women have been socialized to assume primary responsibility for family relationships (Walters, Carter, Papp, & Silverstein, 1988). Traditional Latino gender roles stipulate that females subordinate their individual needs to those of the group. Many Latinas have an extended, collective and contextual definition of themselves. The extended self is validated only by its functioning in relationship and in harmony with the group (Nobles, 1980). The extended self definition posits that women perceive themselves as being individuals within a collective and non-linear context and therefore, their relationships to others and need for individual and collective survival are central to their well being and sense of continuity (Comas-Díaz, in press). Although the concept of well being and the sense of group continuity may appear to enforce traditional gender roles within the family, the extended self promotes a combined instrumental (rational) and expressive (emotional) concept of womanhood prevalent among many women of color (Comas-Díaz, in press).

The family is the major source of socializing cultural values, mores, beliefs, and behaviors. Within this context, the LatiNegra's own family can be a source of both approval and rejection in the form of *racismo*. The family's racial rejection complicates the process of self acceptance for the LatiNegra. For instance, Franklin and Boyd-Franklin (1985) argue that racial socialization is enhanced in the context of love and support for the child, but it is negatively affected when it occurs in the context of parental contempt and rejection, as in the case of many LatiNegras. Consequently, the LatiNegra's self-esteem suffers. The family dynamics often target the LatiNegra for racial exclusion due to the intersection of race and gender. The LatiNegra's individual characteristics are viewed through the lens of female blackness and often acquire negative connotations. For example, a colicky baby may be identified as: *esa prieta majadera* (that bothersome Black female baby) while a non-Black colicky baby may engender concern or be identified as a *majadera*, without any allusion to her color. Since infancy, the LatiNegra learns to associate her blackness with negative attributes. Moreover, during childhood, adolescence, and adulthood she frequently hears parents and family members making racist-sexist remarks towards other LatiNegras.

Internalized racism, colonization, and oppression are often present among many Latinos, particularly among those with visible African ancestry. The dynamics of internalized sexism and racism are frequently channeled at the expense of the LatiNegra. This process becomes heightened when the family has recently immigrated and copes with learning a new culture, language, and racial dynamics. Many Latinos face the *racial cultural shock* which involves being perceived in a racially dichotomous manner (Black or White), being racially discriminated against, subjected to an overt individual and institutionalized racism, and being considered genetically inferior due to their race.

The racial cultural shock may persist even for generations after the family's translocation. In other words, LatiNegras whose families have been in the United States for several years may still be ill equipped to deal with racism. Among Latinos with African ancestry in the United States, feelings about self and others are related to color differences between the LatiNegra and others. Many non-White Latinos, such as *trigueños, jabaos, mulatos,* and *grifos,* experience racial identity diffusion in that within the Latino context they may be considered non-Black, but in the North American context they are perceived as non-White. Consequently, the LatiNegra embodies a painful mirror that non-White Latinos with internalized racism may want to break. She is the reflection of their blackness, and due to her powerlessness resulting from racism, sexism, and classism the LatiNegra is racially excluded. She searches for self-definition at a great risk to herself. Many of these feelings and dynamics often generate destructive relationships between LatiNegras and their siblings, parents, relatives (Thomas, 1967), and friends (Rivera, 1982).

Many Latino families do not have appropriate socialization skills within an overt racist environment. For example, Greene (1990) argues that women who have been confronted early on in life with direct and open racial discrimination, who have had it accurately labeled for what it is, and who have received family support in developing strategies for overcoming and enduring it, may be better prepared to manage racial discrimination later in life. She further adds that women who were forced to address racial discrimination with little or no support, or confronted it in more subtle and indirect forms may be less prepared to address it, and may be at greater risk for internalizing its destructive aspects. The LatiNegra is obviously at a disadvantage due to her lack of family support in coping with racial discrimination as a Black woman. Frequently, the LatiNegra's lack of family support results in a negative self internalization. The pervasiveness of racism and the varied efforts and methods Blacks use to minimize its damaging effects on themselves can be accurately perceived as a major source of stress (Greene, 1990). Many non-

Black Latinos do not experience this type of racial stress and thus, cannot minimize its negative effects on their LatiNegra daughters.

Latino groups and communities are collectively incompetent to deal with the type of racial discrimination confronted by LatiNegros. As previously indicated, the Latinos with African ancestry may find it difficult to accept their own blackness due to their internalized racism and colonialism. Those Latinos with visible African heritage often harbor negative attributions of being Black which are then externalized and projected onto the LatiNegra. In a poignant article describing the experience of being a Puerto Rican LatiNegra, Jorge (1979) asserts that her multiple minority status engenders shame and feelings of inferiority, which are reinforced by the Latino culture and dominant society at large. Unlike an African American female, the LatiNegra cannot expect nor does she receive the protection of her family against racism as a Black female. Moreover, the LatiNegra's mother did not prepare her to become a Black woman by communicating the racial and sexual dangers, stereotypes, and realities that confront Black females, nor how to interpret them, or to cope with them.

Blackness often produces intense ambivalence among Latinos. The personal and collective African heritage makes blackness a part of the self that is both loved and hated. The loving Black *abuela* is a source of both nurturance and shame. The *African queen* may be sexually exciting as a lover, but is rejected as a potential wife. The ambivalence is further concretized in the usage of language, where the same racially derogatory terms such as *negra* and *prieta* are also expressions of affection (Zenón Cruz, 1975). This linguistic usage is similar to the use of the word *Nigger* among some African Americans as a term of familiarity and endearment. Mixed race Latinos also struggle with their own blackness at an intrapsychic level. Their reaction to the LatiNegra frequently involves a confrontation of their own blackness. Such confrontation encompasses intense conflict, shame, and guilt, resulting in the rejection of the LatiNegra. Consider the following vignette.

Antonio, a non-Black Puerto Rican male was married to Ann, a White Anglo Saxon Protestant (WASP) woman. Antonio began an affair with Celia, a LatiNegra of Cuban background. As the relationship unfolded, sexual difficulties began to emerge. On one occasion, Celia experienced sadness (due to the illicit status of their liaison) and began to cry during love making. Antonio trivialized the incident by responding that: *Blacks cry when they are having sex.* This type of defensive reaction is frequently found among individuals with diffused racial identity. As a racially mixed man, Antonio's marriage to Ann may be interpreted as an internalization of the White middle class female beauty ideal. However, having an affair with Celia may indicate ambivalence and a search for a more integrated racial identity. This search, notwithstanding Antonio's insensitive behavior towards Celia, appears to be a reflection of the combination of sexism and racism through the projection of racial and sexual dynamics. As indicated earlier, the projection of *racismo* and of blackness is a racial defense mechanism among many Latinos.

Racial and Sexual Dynamics

LatiNegras are exposed to the mainstream's racism and sexism, in addition to *racismo* and *sexismo* from the Latino community. They are stripped of their humanity, denied their individuality, and devalued. Individual and institutional racism complicate Latinegras' experiences. They are frequently rejected by both the mainstream White and the Latino societies due to their blackness. Such double rejection often leads to the development of solidarity with African Americans. The African American and the LatiNegro community both share the common denominator of being Black in an openly racist society. For most African Americans, racism is an alive expectation requiring adaptation to ongoing levels of stress connected to survival, and inextricably bound up in physical characteristics which are always visible (Greene, 1990). The commonality in the LatiNegra's experiences with those of African Americans facilitates the identification with this group.

Many LatiNegros in the United States adapt and tend to assimilate to the mainstream society as African Americans. In some cases, they may change their accent, adopting a non-standard Black English (del Valle, personal communication, 1993; Seda-Bonilla, 1970). When color supersedes ethnicity and culture as the source of identity for Latinos with African ancestry, they often assimilate into the racial antagonisms of the United States (Longres, 1974). The result is that lighter Latinos may marry White Americans, Latinos or other non-

Black individuals, while darker Latinos will marry African Americans or other Blacks. Consequently, marital liaisons between Lati-Negras and African Americans can be common.

The LatiNegra who marries an African American man often gives birth to non-Latinos. The ultimate outcome of this process is the total assimilation of LatiNegros to the African American group without identifying—socially, emotionally, and politically—with the Latino community (Jorge, 1979). The assimilation into the African American community is aided by the conflict in racial loyalties that many LatiNegros experience when they become members of the African American diaspora. This conflict is illustrated in anecdotal and autobiographical materials. For instance, while discussing his experiences growing up as a Hispanic in Spanish Harlem, Edward Rivera (1982) tells the story of his LatiNegro Puerto Rican friend, Panna, whose African American friends prevented him from interacting with his non-Black Puerto Rican friends *in Black turf*. Such conflict often leads to the LatiNegros' immersion into the African American group at the exclusion of their Latino identification.

SEXUALITY

The intersection of gender and multiraciality involves confronting the oppressive mythology associated with being a mixed race woman (Root, in press). As Black females, LatiNegras often conjure up ideas of exoticism, evil, dark power, sensuality, and strong sexuality. There is no other area that engenders more fantasies than the strong sexuality attributed to the LatiNegra. Within the racist and sexist North American society there is a level of sexual fantasy regarding the possession of and dominance over the sexuality and sexual behavior of women who are unfamiliar to the male (Root, 1992a). The mixed racial woman is considered the stereotypic unusual sexual being (Nakashira, 1992).

The LatiNegra exemplifies the unusual sexual being within the Latino culture. Many Latinos project diverse sexual fantasies onto the LatiNegra. These fantasies mediate LatiNegras' real and assumed sexuality. For example, having sex with a LatiNegra can be considered aphrodisiacal (*afrodisíaco* in Spanish). Moreover, there is the perception that the LatiNegra has no control over her sexuality, and thus, can engender the same effect on her sexual partner, or on the contrary, has an inhibitory effect.

Another fantasy is that the LatiNegra's strong sexuality is transmitted by osmosis. Within the Caribbean Latino community having a LatiNegra lover can be a testament of the man's sexual prowess. For example, a non-Black Puerto Rican man told his Dominican LatiNegra lover: *I like being with you because when men see us together they know that I . . .* (perform cunnilingus) *you.*

Many of these sexual fantasies can transcend the traditional gender roles. For instance, having a LatiNegra lover can heighten fantasies of power and powerlessness, with its dimensions of dominance and submission, enacted in the sexual act. These dynamics can also transcend sexual orientation. Although embodied in a specific sociopolitical context, the effect of race within lesbian relationships can also be subjected to externalization of internalized oppression. Consider the following vignette.

A lesbian couple decided to move in together after six months of dating. Their sexual behavior involved sadomasochistic activities with Áurea, the White Cuban woman, as the active partner. Soon after their move, Áurea began to physically attack Luisa, her LatiNegra Puerto Rican lover. The situation escalated to the point that Luisa gave Áurea an ultimatum. As a result, they entered couples counseling. During the initial session Áurea said: *I will never hit a White lover.* In other words, she was responding to the racial collective unconscious that Blacks have been slaves and thus, deserve to be physically abused. The racist hierarchical attributions of Blacks being inferior to Whites were evident within this dynamic. Moreover, Áurea had internalized the cultural dichotomous attributions of females as being either all good or all bad (Virgin Mary/Eve; Madonna/whore) (Almquist, 1989; Comas-Díaz, 1987). Within this context, the LatiNegra epitomizes the stereotypical bad woman. Further exploration revealed that Áurea had dissociated from her own African ancestry by displacing onto Luisa her internalized racial oppression. Thus, by oppressing Luisa, Áurea was rejecting parts of herself. This dynamic reflects an image whereby identification with the aggressor occurs in a racist, patriarchal, sexist, and heterosexist society.

As the previous vignette suggests, the sexual arena can become the soul's mirror. Many Latinos with mixed racial ancestry often deal with racial ambivalence within themselves. Thus, being sexually involved with a LatiNegra can produce a confrontation with such ambivalence. As an illustration, Juan, a racially mixed Cuban male began a relationship with María, a Cuban LatiNegra. Juan experienced sexual impotence and terminated the relationship with a cry of: *I cannot screw my father!* Regardless of gender and sexual orientation, Juan had identified María with his own LatiNegro father. Consequently, racial identity had transcended gender identity. Juan was plagued by guilt due to immigrating from Cuba and leaving his LatiNegro father behind.

Closely related to the LatiNegra's sexuality is the issue of dark or occult power. Many LatiNegros are attributed the dark power of the occult. For example, Zenón Cruz (1975) argues that people in the Caribbean trust a Black folk healer more than a White one and are more afraid of Black witches than they are of White ones. Consequently, one of the ways for LatiNegros to obtain respect is through the practice of *espiritismo* (spiritualism), *curanderismo* and or *santería*. Females tend to predominate in the area of spiritual healing among Latino communities (Espín, 1984; Mays & Comas-Díaz, 1987). Historically, women in most cultures have resorted to healing and magic as a means of empowerment (Bourguignon, 1979). Similarly, many Latinas, particularly the LatiNegra, gain power through their roles as folk healers such as *curanderas, espiritistas,* and *santeras* (Comas-Díaz, 1988; Espín, 1991; Koss-Chioino, 1992). The Catholic church's hierarchical definition of God as a White male, in addition to the prohibition against women becoming priests, seem to provide an impetus for the proliferation of female healers among many Latinos. The influence of female folk healers can be so pervasive that Boyd-Franklin and García Preto (in press) advise family therapists to consider the Latino family's involvement with *curanderas, santeras,* and *espiritistas.*

In summary, there is a defensiveness among LatiNegras stemming from the oppressive racial and sexual dynamics. Sexually, the LatiNegra is not allowed to be an individual. The paradoxes that surround her life–unattractiveness but strong sexuality; oppression but dark power–all have an effect on the LatiNegra's sense of identity.

IDENTITY

The question of racial ancestry becomes a threat to the LatiNe-gra's identity. She is forced to come to grips with the reality of her racial identity. She is often denied the ability to define herself, which is essential to empowerment (Collins, 1991; Helms, 1990). As a mixed race woman, she is also denied the opportunity to claim membership in and identify with more than one racial or ethnic group (Hall, 1992; Root, 1990). The LatiNegra differs from other mixed racial women in that she does not engender curiosity regarding her racial identity. There are no ambiguous features–she is perceived as being Black. However, like other biracial women, the LatiNegra needs to accept both sides of her racial heritage and has the right to declare how she wishes to identify herself racially–even if this identity is discrepant with how she looks.

The LatiNegra's racial exclusion and her lack of acceptance and belonging to the Latino community is doubly painful. She often experiences a fragmented identity. Multiracial identity can jeopardize the LatiNegra's sense of belonging to a group. For example, Root (in press) argues that a major difference between African Americans and multiracially identified African Americans (such as LatiNegras) is not necessarily their racial heritage, but that the latter group of people identify as multicultural and feel a kinship with more than one group. However such identification may also be related to a desire to passing as non-Black by not identifying with the group of lowest racial and social standing (African Americans). For instance, Almeida (personal communication, 1993) asserts that some dark skinned Asian Indians would prefer to be mistaken for Latinos than Blacks. Nonetheless, it is vital for the LatiNegra to be able to identify with multiple groups, particularly with the Latino and the African.

Attribution of the Other is a dynamic highly relevant to the LatiNegra's identity. Otherness refers to the process whereby an individual's attribution of people of different ethnocultural background helps the person to define his or her own concept of self. For instance, women in the general population have been described as men's Other in that they are defined in reference to men and not men in reference to women (de Beauvoir, 1961). Moreover, Kovel (1984) asserts that Europeans' fantasies about Africans and American Indians helped the former to define themselves. Similarly, Jenkins (1985) has argued that for White Americans, people of color may be a cultural representation of the polar opposite. The notion of Other creates a dichotomous thinking and objectification, where difference is defined in oppositional terms. The dynamics of color and racial projection create a dramatic polarity, the projection of the not-me (Collins, 1990). The Other gains meaning only in relationship to the counterpart (Fanon, 1967).

Women of color have been identified as the Other's Other in terms of being the man of color's Other and the White woman's Other (Comas-Díaz, 1991). Collins (1991) believes that maintaining images of African American women as the Other provides ideological justification for race, gender, and class oppression. This justification can be generalized to include LatiNegras, in that they are doubly marginalized and racially excluded within their own group as well as being outsiders in the population as a whole. As the target of sexual-racial projection, the LatiNegra is the paragon of Otherness. She is not self-defined, instead, she is defined by others. Consequently, she often copes with severe identity conflicts. If she only identifies as a Latina, she denies her blackness. If she only identifies as a Black, she denies her Latinness. Denial of one aspect of her identity implies denial of the self and heritage, plus sacrifice of personal integrity (Mizio, 1982).

LatiNegras' identification with a single group involves an ethno-racial denial as well as a psychocultural denial. Although the denial of ethno-racial identity may be a racial coping mechanism, it also leaves the denier vulnerable to loneliness, personal isolation, political powerlessness, and devoid of the opportunity to correct and transcend distorted ethno-racial perceptions of the group and of herself (Greene, 1992). The ethno-racial denial fosters a psychocultural denial of the self. By identifying exclusively with one group, the LatiNegra renounces herself by replacing a multiracial identity with a single racial one. Consequently, one of the LatiNegra's fundamental tasks is to preserve herself by affirming and integrating her multi-ethnic and racial identity. Many times her fragmented identity surfaces during mental health treatment and needs to be addressed in that arena.

The LatiNegra spends an inordinate amount of energy in her

ongoing struggle with the mainstream group's and Latino's racial, gender and ethnic prejudices. Like other mixed race women, the LatiNegra does not necessarily identify racially with her physical appearance or with the way she looks (Black). She is caught between three diverse (and sometimes, antagonistic) worlds–Black, Latino, and White–and racially excluded from all. Her marginality binds her in a conflict of racial loyalties without a satisfactory resolution of her racial identity.

Physical Appearance

Physical appearance is a central component of female identity in a patriarchal and sexist society. As indicated previously, among many Latin Caribbean societies race is related to class and thus, it can be more flexible and fluid. For example, a LatiNegra from a higher socioeconomic class (although this is highly infrequent due to the Caribbean historical connection between blackness and low socioeconomic class) is not socially perceived as being Black, instead she may be perceived as "morena" or "trigueña." Social class, the dictum of *adelantar la raza* still govern the LatiNegra's physical appearance and her suitability for marriage. The constructs of colonization and internalized colonization add to the objectification of the LatiNegra, who often represents the antithesis of the White male colonizer.

The issue of physical appearance is a pervasive theme among mixed race women (Root, in press). The LatiNegra's physical appearance is often a target of racism and covert *racismo*. Regardless of color, males and females in the United States are immersed in and intoxicated by White female beauty standards. Due to pervasive media influence, many African American females, African Caribbean females, and LatiNegras grow up with a fantasy of aspiring to be White (as girls they are forced to identify with Snow White or Barbie, and as young and adult women, with White fashion models or those non-White models who have Caucasian features). These dynamics can result in hopelessness about their physical appearance and self hatred due to their blackness.

In the Latin Caribbean, the covert nature of *racismo* is also illustrated in the female beauty standards. Blackness (dark color, Black features, kinky hair, and body shape) tends to have implications for attractiveness only, and not necessarily for racial inferiority. Although the LatiNegra is not considered intellectually inferior, she is definitively considered unattractive. The LatiNegra's physical appearance is the antithesis of physical desirability and attractiveness among many Caribbean Latinos. According to Longres (1974), to be *rubia* (blond or fair) and/or with light eyes is esthetically prized. He adds that straight hair is considered an indication of beauty, while *pelo malo* (literally bad hair, refers to kinky hair) is generally considered the ugliest and most condemning feature a person may have. As an illustration, the racial categorizations of *grifa* and *jabá* attribute blackness primarily based on the texture of the hair (kinky).

The denial and rejection of the LatiNegra's female blackness have serious implications for her self-esteem. Non-White Latinas such as *trigueñas, grifas, morenas,* and *indias* may externalize their internalized racism by attempting to whiten themselves through torturing their hair and scalp by chemically straightening their *bad* kinky hair; by using bleaching creams; and generally trying to look less Black. Although these attempts carry high physical and emotional costs, these non-White Latinas appear to have more degrees of freedom in terms of their racial identity compared to LatiNegras who cannot modify their blackness. However, many LatiNegras resort to an arsenal of weapons to attempt to whiten themselves, often resulting in pain, frustration, and hopelessness. Some LatiNegras may engage in torturing and life threatening activities such as the eleven-year-old girl who was taken unconscious to the hospital emergency room after using a clothes pin to close her wide nose in order to make it narrow and thus, look less Black.

The LatiNegra is resented and rejected due to her blackness, which is often defined as kinky hair, thick lips, wide hips, and dark color. Blackness evokes expressions of ridicule, rejection, and hostility. Female blackness, with its compounded racism and sexism, is often a target for negative remarks, even from significant others. Jorge (1979) provides several of these painful examples. For instance, the demand: *Cierra esa bemba!* (Close your mouth!) commands the LatiNegra to avoid leaving her lower lip (generally thicker lip) hanging. (The word *bemba* is a pejorative term referring to a thick lipped mouth.) As a child, the LatiNegra often suffers insults to her self-esteem from a loved caretaker. For example, while her hair is being combed by a mother or maternal figure, the expressions: *Maldito sea este pelo!* (Damn this hair!), or *Dios mío, este pelo!* (Dear God, this hair!) engender feelings of inadequacy, unattractiveness (Jorge 1979), and self-hatred.

MENTAL HEALTH ISSUES

Self-Esteem in the Extended Context

The LatiNegra's socioculturally imposed identity conflict affects her self-esteem. Being multiracial in itself poses no inherent type of stress that would result in psychological maladjustment; however, the distress related to being multicultural is likely to be a response to an environment that has internalized racist beliefs (Root, in press). This type of distress stems from oppression and is frequently metamorphosed into low self-esteem.

The LatiNegra's self-esteem problem is exacerbated by the identification of multiracial individuals as the racial and/or ethnic group with lower perceived status by the higher status group. Although both African Americans and Latinos have a low social status within the North American society, the history of racism and White supremacy tends to assign even a lower status to those individuals who look Black (Root, in press). Due to her socially imposed low self-esteem and inferior social standing, the LatiNegra experiences powerlessness and learned helplessness.

The politics and dynamics of race, gender and class add to the singularity and uniqueness of the LatiNegra, threatening her identity and sense of continuity, thus, further eroding her self-esteem. The stressful and traumatic circumstances surrounding the lives of Lati-Negras are compounded by the racism and sexism from both the Latino and mainstream communities. Being considered at least three minorities in one–Black, Latina, and female–is a tremendous psychological burden that needs to be understood (Jorge, 1979) and addressed, particularly in the therapeutic process. Consequently, LatiNegras' membership in multiple minority groups often engenders their identity, decreasing their self-esteem.

Trauma

LatiNegras experience a multiplicity of trauma. They confront trauma at historic-political, transgenerational, psychosocial, and personal levels. LatiNegras' history of societal and political trauma includes slavery, oppression and subjugation as Black females. The historic-political context of their racial and gender exclusions constitute ancestral traumatic events which are embedded in Lati-Negras' collective unconscious. Moreover, this historical trauma is the precursor of contemporary racial and sexual discrimination in the midst of hostile environments. The cumulative dose of discrimination may become so toxic that the processes of denial or suppression are similar to those in post traumatic stress disorder (PTSD) where emotional flooding and disorganized behavior can be triggered by subtle clues, reminders, or even mini instances of what has been suppressed (Hamilton, 1989). Similarly, Vásquez (in press) argues that Latinas' chronic exposure to racism can lead to powerlessness, learned helplessness, depression, anxiety, and PTSD. This traumatic situation is exacerbated for LatiNegras, who confront multiple societal and psychosocial barriers due to their assigned inferior status dictated by gender, race, ethnicity, and class.

LatiNegras are further exposed to what Root (1992b) calls insidious trauma, or the cumulative effect of racism, sexism, dislocation, and other types of oppression. She argues that insidious trauma is frequently associated with the low social status attributed to individuals who are devalued because they are different from those in power due to an intrinsic identity characteristic such as gender, race, or sexual orientation. As members of multiple powerless minority groups, LatiNegras often become a target for racial, gender, and class victimization. As indicated previously, LatiNegras are oppressed and victimized through racial and sexual exclusions by the dominant group as well as by their own communities.

LatiNegras are also exposed to transgenerational trauma. Given their families' powerlessness and absence of racial and gender socialization, this trauma and victimization cycle perpetuates itself from one generation of LatiNegras to the next. The lack of societal and psychocultural reparation for the LatiNegra within the Latino community reinforces the transgenerational trauma. The LatiNegra's transgenerational trauma has a psychosocial component. The trauma inflicted by their own communities and families creates a psychosocial victimization. Due to internalized racism, the rejection from the LatiNegra's own group results in disempowerment and fosters her internalization of negative views of herself. Thus, the LatiNegra is unable to racially socialize her daughter as a Black female and to convey to her a positive sense of self.

Many LatiNegras experience added trauma at a personal level. They confront several traumatas in their lives which leave indelible effects on their functioning and self-esteem. Traumata refers to the series of little traumas or events that when coupled with general life stresses and reduced environmental and psychological resources can bring the LatiNegra to the traumatic stress flashpoint (Puig, 1991). The message that LatiNegras are inferior due to their combination of gender, race, ethnicity, and class further adds to their victimization. This type of victimization acquires a sense of progression. Powerlessness breeds more powerlessness. Unfortunately, many LatiNegras are caught in a cycle of oppression, discrimination, trauma and victimization, and are often subjected to revictimization.

TREATMENT APPROACHES

Effective mental health treatment necessitates addressing the unique circumstances of the LatiNegra. Due to the multiplicity of oppressions and trauma, an empowerment framework is crucial to address LatiNegras' mental health needs. An empowerment perspective such as a feminist orientation helps LatiNegras to: (1) acknowledge the deleterious combined effects of racism, sexism, and classism; (2) deal with negative feelings imposed by their status as LatiNegras; (3) understand the interplay between external environment and their inner reality; (4) negotiate conflictive cultural demands; (5) perceive themselves as causal agents in achieving solutions to their problems (Comas-Díaz, 1987; Mays & Comas-Díaz, 1988; & Solomon, 1982); and, (6) address their fragmented racial and gender identity.

Feminist values are particularly relevant for LatiNegras. The feminist emphasis on the equalization of power can help LatiNegras to address their powerlessness by recognizing the need for and the development of more egalitarian relationships. The feminist belief that women have had limited choices as a result of their oppression and that internalized negative self-beliefs stem from such oppression, can help LatiNegras to combat low self-esteem. Moreover, the feminist principle that the personal is political can help LatiNegras to cope and work towards the transformation of their oppressive realities, potentially enabling them to achieve more control over their lives. Similarly, the feminist value of social action follows from the belief that women's problems are based in a societal as well as in a personal context.

An empowerment orientation needs to integrate an external perspective with an examination of internal reality. On an inner level, LatiNegras require corrective learning experiences, in order to acquire new functional coping skills. Given LatiNegras' exposure to multiple trauma, cognitive behavioral approaches are helpful in challenging their victim mentality and increasing their self-determination. These techniques constitute tools for correcting cognitive errors caused by victim mentality. This approach is highly relevant for LatiNegras, because their cognitive errors reinforce their victim mentality by mirroring the hopelessness, helplessness, sense of betrayal, and low self-esteem resulting from trauma. A victim mentality involves (1) intolerance of mistakes in self and others; (2) denial of personal difficulties; (3) dichotomous thinking; and, (4) continuation of survival tactics (Matsakis, 1992).

LatiNegras' conflicted and fragmented identity and consequent lowered self-esteem are major mental health issues. Thus, addressing LatiNegras' fragmented identity is a primary aspect of their mental health treatment. Narrative (story) approaches can be auxiliary therapeutic techniques to address the development of racial and gender identity as a life-story construction (Howard, 1991). The re-construction of the LatiNegra's life story can be empowering and healing. Similarly, in working with victims, Matsakis (1992) recommends the rewriting of the story of the trauma with a different ending as a healing technique.

Another narrative approach empowering to LatiNegras is the cultural story. The cultural story refers to an ethnocultural group's origins, migration, and identity (McGill, 1992). At the family level, the cultural story is used to tell where the ancestors came from, what kind of people they were, what issues are important, and what lessons have been learned from their experience. These specific tasks are significantly relevant to the special needs of LatiNegras. Discussing family stories involving Black female protagonists can build and enhance self-esteem among LatiNegras, by learning from other Black women's struggles, triumphs, and defeats. LatiNegras' victimized racial and gender identity needs to be rescued, reclaimed, and celebrated through the narration and reconstruction of their life stories.

Asking women of color about their mothers' stories can be another helpful clinical technique in addressing identity issues (Comas-Díaz, in press). Within this context, in working with LatiNegras I often explore the client's stories about her mother, surrogate mothers, or other Black females' stories. Although I do not provide specific guidelines, I often ask the LatiNegra to describe her female role models to a stranger, her recollections of these female figures when they were the client's current age, how they exhibited gender and racial roles, plus how they dealt with sexism, racism, and particularly, racial oppression as LatiNegras. If the mother is not a LatiNegra, I ask the client to comment on their similarities and differences. This line of questioning can reveal identity conflicts, thus facilitating working towards the integration of a fragmented racial-gender identity.

Given the extended self-concept prevalent among many LatiNegras, family therapy is highly congruent with their reality. For Latinas and African American women the family is often the principal support system and the source of help during crisis. Boyd-Franklin and Garcia Preto (in press) assert that family therapy lends itself in a very positive way to the treatment of these women and their families as a therapeutic modality and as a conceptual understanding of change. These authors further postulate that family therapy with one person is a culturally congruent approach with African American women and Latinas due to their strong family and extended family ties. Consequently, when family members are not available for treatment due to economic burdens, the format of family therapy with one person can be extremely useful.

Family therapists who do not challenge the ideal gender roles that inform their clinical interventions tend to maintain the status quo by perpetuating traditional and restrictive sex roles (Bograd,

1988). Therefore, it is important to recognize the effects of the gender and race interaction in family therapy. Similarly, we need to examine the metamessages conveyed to the woman by a specific family therapy intervention (Walters et al., 1988). For instance, while coaching a woman of color, the family therapist needs to avoid the sexist underlying assignment of over responsibility and blame for family problems to the woman (Almeida, personal communication, 1993).

A feminist family therapy approach is helpful and compatible with the LatiNegra's collective and contextual cultural orientation. For example, Walters and her associates (1988) revise family therapy from a feminist perspective, arguing that all interventions need to take gender into account, recognizing the different socialization processes of women and men, and paying special attention to the way in which these socialization processes disadvantage women. However, in working with LatiNegras feminist family therapy approaches need to take more than gender into account. They need to examine the effects of both racism and sexism. One construct cannot be overemphasized at the expense of the other. For example, many family therapists of color may prefer not to address gender directly, because they identify racism as the pervasive oppressor (Almeida, personal communication, 1993). Such an assertion goes along with the identification of race as the social variable that transcends and intensifies the effects of gender, sexual orientation, class, religion, and others among people of color (Cole, 1986; Ladner, 1971). Notwithstanding these assertions, the lives of women of color need to be examined from a racial minority-feminist perspective, one that recognizes that not only both racism and sexism exist and are equally oppressive to women of color, but also their combination is oppressive to women of color. Similarly, Gould (1985) argues that racism and sexism interact to produce gender-specific race effects and race-specific gender effects which need to be stressed apart from the separate effects of racism and sexism in the lives of women of color and their children. The gender-specific race effects and the race-specific gender effects comprise the fabric of the lives of LatiNegras.

The use of multigenerational genogram (McGoldrick & Gerson, 1985), prevalent among family therapy approaches, can be particularly relevant for LatiNegras when issues of gender and race are examined and highlighted. Moreover, the use of a cultural transitional map (Ho, 1987) also proves to be effective in enhancing LatiNegras' self-esteem. The cultural transitional map assesses personal, familial, ethno-cultural, and community mappings in families who undergo rapid social change and cultural transition (Ho, 1987). It involves the collection of personal, psychological, social, and cultural data, in addition to the assessment of the transitional position and family developmental stages of the multigenerational family in a changing society. Clinical techniques include the use of photographs, albums, paintings, and native music, in addition to the standard questions and answers mode (Ho, 1987). The cultural transitional map can be used to identify color and gender issues and conflicts between the LatiNegra and her family members. These therapeutic approaches will be addressed in the following case vignette.

YAMILA'S STORY:
A JOURNEY OF LOSS, RECONSTRUCTION,
AND CELEBRATION

Presenting Problems and Identifying Data

Yamila, a 35-year-old Cuban LatiNegra, lived with her mother and a 9-year-old daughter. She was involved in a romantic relationship with a Latino (Dominican) man and was working as an assistant administrator in a federal government agency. The client was referred to mental health treatment by an Employee Assistance Program due to insubordination against her supervisor and a series of chronic interpersonal problems with her co-workers.

Yamila was referred to a mixed race Latina therapist. She reacted positively to her clinician and commented on their shared Latino Caribbean background. Yamila appeared to the therapist as very angry and stated that she had been the scapegoat of her office. Upon exploration of this assertion, she expressed that she was mistreated because she was a Black Latina and her co-workers were African Americans and her supervisor was a high yellow African American woman.

Racial and gender dynamics seemed to dominate Yamila's work

history. For instance, she felt racially excluded by her colleagues at the workplace. She admitted to depressive symptoms–depressed mood, irritability and hostility, difficulties falling asleep, in addition to interpersonal difficulties with her relatives, friends, and co-workers. Yamila had suicidal ideations without active plans and denied any substance use. She acknowledged a connection between her anger and her depression, and agreed to work on this in therapy.

Gender and Racial Dynamics

Yamila's genogram revealed that she was the middle of three siblings, with an older brother (2 years older) and a younger sister (one year younger). In discussing her childrearing, Yamila stated that as the oldest female, she was responsible for mothering her siblings when her mother was absent. While Yamila was growing up, she was close to her maternal grandmother. This type of relationship with her grandmother represents a positive cultural choice frequently available in Latino families. After the Cuban revolution, Yamila's father obtained a relatively high position in the government due to his participation in the revolution. Afterwards, he was accused of being antirevolutionary and was removed from his position, and as a punishment, was sent to cut sugarcane. This situation marked a significant change in Yamila's family. They went from having a somewhat privileged position, to being ostracized by the government. Yamila remembers this incident as a shattering one in her life.

After several attempts, the family was able to move from Cuba. However, her maternal grandparents were unable to leave, and this generated feelings of guilt among the family members, particularly in Yamila. She was 14-years-old and her adjustment to the United States was a very difficult one due to both culture and racial shock. Her father was employed as a security guard and her mother worked as a domestic helper. Yamila and her sister began to experience interpersonal difficulties. The family had no relatives in the United States and did not socialize with other Cubans due to the father's previous political associations with the revolution. However, they soon discovered that their difficulties were primarily because of color rather than political issues.

Color Issues

Yamila, her daughter, father, and brother were LatiNegros. Her mother was *trigueña* and her sister was *grifa.* Her maternal grandmother was LatiNegra while her grandfather was *indio.* Her paternal grandparents had died a long time ago and they were reported to be LatiNegros. While in Cuba, the family had a sense of belonging to other non-White and LatiNegro Cuban families. But in the United States, they encountered difficulties socializing.

The immigration and subsequent cultural transition and translocation significantly affected Yamila's sense of self. She was identified as Black while her sister, who was a *grifa,* was identified as a Latina. As a result people did not believe that they were sisters: *You two cannot be sisters.* Additionally, different than her sister, Yamila was subjected to numerous racial discriminations such as going to swimming pools where her light skinned sister was allowed to enter and she was denied entrance. Her mother began to favor her *grifa* sister in terms of going shopping (for English translation purposes) in order to avoid racial discrimination. This favoritism extended to other areas as well, creating severe problems between Yamila and her mother. Her own difficulties with her sister were also related to these color dynamics. Meanwhile, her LatiNegro brother became immersed in the African American community and received minimal reaction from the family. However, when Yamila began to befriend African Americans, her mother reacted very negatively, prohibiting her to go out with Black friends. This reaction underscores the family's differential treatment to a LatiNegra daughter as opposed to a LatiNegro son. Consequently, Yamila, who was fully bilingual, began to speak with a Spanish accent in order to differentiate herself from African Americans.

Sexuality

Yamila's physical appearance was validated by African American men. Back in Cuba, her physical appearance was validated by the interest of several men. Indeed, Yamila was a very attractive woman, but saw herself as ugly. Moreover, she was rejected by Latino and White men. While her sister was dating Latinos, Yamila began to date African Americans. At age 18 she became pregnant and her boyfriend wanted to marry her, but her parents opposed such a marriage. This incident created a major conflict between Yamila and her mother. However, due to family pressures, cultural expectations, loyalty issues, and external realities, Yamila obeyed her parents and terminated her relationship with her African American boyfriend. She gave birth to her daughter, Jazmín, and went to business school while her mother took care of Jazmín. Around this time, her father was murdered while he was working as a night security guard. This loss was a traumatic one for Yamila, who was the father's favorite. Within the same year Yamila's sister married a Puerto Rican man and moved to Puerto Rico. Due to these losses, and for financial reasons, her mother moved in with Yamila.

Yamila's relationship with her Latino lover was a source of both support and stress. The relationship had been a stable one, lasting for four years. However, during the last year the lover lost his job and had been unemployed ever since then. He was a *trigueño* Dominican and Yamila felt that the relationship was non-egalitarian due to their color differences. Yamila's mother expressed concerns about the relationship due to the financial implications of the lover's unemployment. This situation added to the tension between Yamila and her mother.

Treatment

Yamila and her therapist agreed on addressing the symptom (depression) while simultaneously working on the underlying problem (anger and low self-esteem). Yamila's anger and depression were analyzed as a response to her history of trauma, victimization, and oppression. Among some feminist scholars, female depression has been identified as part of the possible sequelae of trauma and victimization (Hamilton & Jensvold, 1992). Within this context, therapy acknowledged Yamila's history of loss and trauma, and emphasizing her resourcefulness, the survival aspects of her behavior, plus the adaptability of many of her responses to trauma.

Treatment addressed Yamila's feelings of powerlessness and unhappiness. An empowerment psychotherapeutic perspective was used to help Yamila deal with her negative feelings imposed by her status as a LatiNegra. A feminist family therapy orientation was useful in helping Yamila understand the interplay between the external forces of racism and sexism, her family dynamics, and her inner reality. Her conflict at work paralleled her conflict with her sister and mother due to race and gender. This awareness helped Yamila recognize and separate her internal dynamics from the external factors of racism, sexism, discrimination, and glass ceiling at the workplace.

The special meaning of race and gender and their combination in Yamila's family were uncovered using the genogram and the transitional map. These techniques uncovered more personal strengths. For example, Yamila brought in some family photographs, but due to the sudden nature of her immigration, she stated that most of her belongings (including photographs) were left in Cuba. The feminist therapeutic approach helped Yamila to identify new areas of coping with loss. She began to draw portraits of her relatives and friends instead of the missing photographs. Much to her surprise, her family was delighted at her *discovered* talent. Moreover, the process of drawing made Yamila "interview" her family members, creating a focus-oriented and dynamic communication between them.

An analysis of Yamila's multigenerational genogram and her transitional map additionally revealed that LatiNegras have had a central role as healers. In every generation, LatiNegras were not only the family healers but were recognized as folk healers by their communities. Being a healer represented LatiNegras' coping with powerlessness and oppression as Black females. Within this context, LatiNegras had enjoyed significant amount of power inside and outside their family. However, the family cultural myth stated that misfortune will happen to the LatiNegra who does not exercise her role as a healer. Indeed, not performing the feminine role as a folk healer is considered a source of illness among some Latinas (Koss-Chioino, 1992).

As a means of increasing Yamila's functioning and power, treatment focused on reducing her depressive symptomatology. Within this context, she was referred for a psychopharmacological consultation within an empowerment approach tailored for women of color. Such approach addresses the triangulation of treatment (a physician psychopharmacology, a non-physician clinician, and the client) by focusing on ethnocultural and gender factors and on viewing education as an emancipatory psychosocial method aimed at helping women of color manage their situation in a self-affirming manner (Comas-Díaz & Jacobsen, in press).

Cognitive behavioral techniques such as culturally relevant assertiveness training (Comas-Díaz & Duncan, 1985) and relaxation techniques were utilized for stress management. Yamila's victim mentality cognitions were identified. One major negative mindset was her intolerance of mistakes, which created severe difficulties with her co-workers, leading to perfectionist values. Demanding perfection from herself and others resulted in interpersonal difficulties and decreased self-worth. Yamila also experienced dichotomous (all or nothing) thinking. Her dichotomous thinking involved believing that people were either her friends or her enemies, without a medium ground. For example, her Black co-workers were bad, while racially mixed Latino friends were good. Yamila's negative cognitions were systematically challenged and encouraged to change. She responded positively to the cognitive behavioral approaches. They helped Yamila to define her sense of self in the context of treatment.

Mother's Story

Yamila was invited to tell her mother's story. However, she made a different choice, instead, and decided to present her grandmother's story. To choose, rather than passively accept (even your therapist's suggestions) requires power. Choosing in feminist therapy is empowering and means not only choosing power but also choosing how to use it. Yamila was closer to her maternal grandmother, who as another LatiNegra, had experiences dealing with racial and sexual discrimination and objectification. The major themes in her grandmother's story were strength, power, wisdom, sacrifice, and caring. Indeed, her grandmother had been a well known *santera* (folk healer). *Santería* is an Afro Cuban religion that combines the beliefs of the African (Yoruba) *Orichas* with the Catholic Saints (Bernal & Gutierrez, 1988). The *santero(a)* is the priest dedicated to the cult of *Orichas* who also functions as a healer and diviner.

Yamila identified her lack of power as a woman, and particularly as a LatiNegra, as a problem within her relationships with significant others. This assessment was fed back to her in the form of her family's (and consequently her mother's) loss of power and subsequent reactions to political and societal oppression. As part of telling her mother's story and reconstructing Yamila's own story, she was asked to invite her mother in a session. The dyadic session revolved around parenting Yamila's daughter, Jazmín. A multigenerational approach was used, examining the role of women in the family.

Yamila was surprised when her mother agreed to attend successive treatment sessions after the initial one. Therapy focused on enhancing communication and decision making skills, and on fostering support systems for both mother and daughter. Additionally, these interventions were framed to preserve Yamila's and her mother's self-esteem. The interventions were delivered respecting Yamila and her mother's views of their own roles. The issue of multiple trauma and losses–dramatic change in Yamila's family's life-style, immigration, culture and racial shock, father's death, and losing Jazmín's father–was primary during these sessions. Within this context, Yamila experienced an unresolved grief reaction to her father's murder. She seemed to be stuck in the anger stage of mourning as a way of keeping connected to her father. Moreover, anger and grief are intimately connected for many trauma survivors (Matsakis, 1992). Individual and collective grief with her mother empowered both women to accept their grief. The dyadic sessions helped them to develop a mutual support system around grieving. The mourning process also involved a socio-political analysis of violence in communities of color.

Therapy helped both Yamila and her mother to examine critically the effects of oppression, in addition to racism, sexism, their combined effects and internalization in their lives. For example, the mother-daughter-granddaughter relationship was examined within a historical-political context. This examination helped Yamila to see her mother's behavior in a more contextualized manner, given her position in a patriarchal, sexist, and racist society. Conversely, it helped her mother to see the unique effects of racism and sexism on LatiNegras as opposed to Latinas. Jazmín became the common denominator that bonded their experiences as oppressed women. By viewing their lives in a female progression, both women decided to empower themselves by focusing on Jazmín, the newest member of the progression. Subsequent sessions included discussions of process teaching racial and gender socialization to Jazmín as a LatiNe-gra. This allowed Yamila's mother to reexperience mothering, in the context of parenting Jazmín. The work of these women exemplifies the resourcefulness inherent in many women of color.

The Therapeutic Relationship

The therapeutic relationship was a significant element in Yamila's treatment. The initial stages of the therapeutic relationship were characterized by Yamila being pleased with the commonalities she shared with her therapist and the success of the cognitive behavioral techniques helped the therapeutic alliance grow strong. On her mind, Yamila connected her therapist with her maternal grandmother. She also identified her mixed race therapist as being *grifa*, and thus was able to empathize with her realities as a LatiNegra.

As part of the assessment and treatment the clinician examined the potential areas of overlap and conflict in the therapeutic relationship, focussing on ethno-racial and gender considerations. This examination yielded some significant similarities. Both therapist and client were women of color, with a Latino Caribbean background, and with a rainbow ethnic heritage. Like Yamila, the therapist had personal experience with ethno-cultural translocation, loss, cultural-racial shock, and adaptation. The commonalities enhanced the development of credibility and trust, thus, cementing the therapeutic alliance.

The management of the therapeutic relationship was crucial in Yamila's therapy. One therapeutic task was to address Yamila's feelings of exclusion and marginality. The therapeutic relationship focused on empowering Yamila as a LatiNegra. Through an egalitarian perspective and an acceptance of Yamila's reality, the therapeutic relationship helped her to understand the sociopolitical and collective circumstances of LatiNegras' experiences. Within this context, a therapeutic task was to acknowledge and express anger in a functional manner. This objective was magnified around the time of the dyadic meeting with her mother. Yamila became anxious and told her therapist that she was afraid that the therapist would *take her mother's side.* The therapist took at face value this concern and did not address the external and internal oppressive realities mediating LatiNegras' relationships with significant others.

In differentiating herself from the familial and cultural realities of oppression, Yamila's anxiety shifted to anger. Exploration revealed that Yamila's personal reactions toward the therapist were split between feelings of closeness and loyalty, together with some distance and ambivalence, reflecting a triangulation from her family of origin. These differences in her emotional connection to the therapist could easily be traced to the triangulated conflict she experienced between her mother/grandmother and her sister. In other words, she initially identified her therapist with her maternal grandmother, but later identified her with sister. The therapist, like her sister was a *grifa,* and Yamila expected her to abandon her and ally with her mother, just like her sister did when they moved to the United States.

Treatment helped Yamila to identify her expectations regarding the therapist as part of her family script. They were also labelled as part of Yamila's dichotomous thinking. The therapist helped Yamila to directly express her anger, hurt and disappointment at her. She modeled a behavior of validating Yamila's feelings and at the same time, did not abandon her by becoming guarded or defensive. Following the feminist value of the therapist as a role model, the therapeutic relationship was presented as a representation of her relationship with her mother and sister who were powerless and could not protect Yamila from racial oppression. Similarly, assessment of the societal role of racism and sexism helped Yamila understand her mother's and sister's behavior within this context.

Yamila's Story

This work with Yamila was aimed at helping her to develop a new self story. It also attempted to integrate her fragmented racial and gender identity. Such reconstruction included the examination of the family's stories which involved their hopes and aspirations particularly after the translocation. Yamila was surprised to hear from her mother that in the family folklore, Yamila was considered the intelligent one, and that a significant part of the tension between them was due to her mother's disappointment at Yamila's lack of achievement. This discovery was catalytic in Yamila's identification with positive aspects of herself. Within this context, the treatment emphasized the recognition and utilization of Yamila's strengths such as her cognitive capabilities, emotional resourcefulness, perseverance, and family corrections-adaptiveness.

Individual coaching was aimed at restoring and increasing Yamila's functioning. Her anger was reframed as a healthy, legitimate, and realistic response to trauma and loss. She is not unlike many women of color who are frequently in contact with their anger due to combined exposure to racism and sexism. Treatment helped Yamila to differentiate between destructive and non-destructive expressions of anger and loss. She was coached to mobilize her anger into social action. Yamila decided to become socially active and successfully organized a group of mothers in her community to fight drug abuse.

Yamila identified drug abuse among people of color as a coping mechanism against the powerlessness present in their communities. Within this framework she developed a grassroots program to empower mothers and their children. Her community program addressed drug abuse through education and preventive approaches. It was designed to be culturally sensitive to both Latino and African American communities and through this work, Yamila was able to reclaim her multi-generational heritage as a healer. Yamila was in therapy for one year and a half. The major therapeutic themes involved her sense of self, including her identity as a LatiNegra, her relationships with significant others, and her multiple losses. At the time of termination, Yamila was no longer experiencing depression. She had completed the bereavement of her multiple losses and was able to better use her strengths and resources.

Treatment Termination

Yamila was in therapy for one year and a half. The major therapeutic themes involved her sense of self, including her identity as a LatiNegra, her relationships with significant others, and her multiple losses. At the time of termination, Yamila was no longer experiencing depression. She has completed the bereavement of her multiple losses and was able to better use her strengths and resources. Her community work had been so successful that her program was awarded a grant for the prevention of drug abuse among African American and Latino youths. Yamila had resigned her job to become the full time director of the program.

RECONSTRUCTION OF THE LATINEGRA

I have introduced the issues surrounding the LatiNegra, who constitutes a classic example of racial exclusion, marginality, and disconnection. She is caught between three diverse worlds–Black, Latino, and White–and racially excluded from all. Her marginality binds her in a conflict of ethno-racial loyalties without a satisfactory resolution of her identity. The paradoxes that surround her life–unattractiveness but strong sexuality; oppression but dark power–all have an effect on the LatiNegra's sense of identity. Consequently, the LatiNegra often suffers from identity conflicts and needs to integrate her fragmented identity within her cultural and familial contexts in order to combat guilt, shame, and feelings of inferiority engendered by her combined racial-ethnic and gender status. The denial of one aspect of her identity implies denial of the self, her mixed race heritage, and her cultural continuity.

LatiNegras' unique experiences are often framed in a collective context of intense ambivalence, racial projection, resentment, plus racial and gender stereotyping. One of the LatiNegra's fundamental tasks is to preserve herself by integrating and affirming her dual racial and gender identity. The reconstruction of the LatiNegra involves healing the trauma and her wounded sense of self through the reclaiming and celebration of her prismatic racial, ethnic, and gender identity. Feminist family therapy approaches that incorporate collective elements are best equipped to deal with the unique circumstances of LatiNegras.

REFERENCES

Almquist, E. (1989). The experience of minority women in the United States. In J. Freeman (Ed.), *Women: A feminist perspective,* 4th edition, Mountain View, CA: Mayfield Publishing.

Bernal, G. & Gutierrez, M. (1988). Cubans. In L. Comas-Díaz & E.E.H. Griffith (Eds.), *Clinical guidelines in cross cultural mental health.* New York: Wiley & Sons.

Bograd, M. (1988). Power, gender, and the family: Feminist perspectives on family therapy theory. In M.A. Dutton-Douglas & L.E. Walker (Eds.), *Feminist psychotherapies: Integration of therapeutic and feminist systems.* Norwood, New Jersey: Ablex Publishing.

Bourguignon, E. (1979). *A world of women: Anthropological studies of women in societies of the world.* New York: Praeger.

Boyd-Franklin, N. & García Preto, N. (in press). Family therapy: The case of African American and Hispanic women. In L. Comas-Díaz & B. Greene (Eds.), *Women of color and mental health.* New York: Guilford Press.

Cole, J.B. (1986). Commonalities and differences. In J.B. Cole (Ed.), *All American women: Lines that divide, Ties that bind.* New York: Free Press.

Collins, P.H. (1991). *Black feminist thought: Knowledge, consciousness, and the politics of empowerment.* New York: Routledge, Chapman & Hall, Inc.

Comas-Díaz, L. (1987). Feminist therapy with Hispanic/Latina Women: Myth or reality. *Women & Therapy, 6,* 39-61.

Comas-Díaz, L. (1989). Puerto Rican women's cross cultural transitions: Developmental and clinical implications. In C. Garcia Coll & M.L. Mattei (Eds.), *The psychosocial development of Puerto Rican women.* New York: Praeger.

Comas-Díaz, L. (1991). Feminism and diversity in psychology: The case of women of color. *Psychology of Women Quarterly, 15,* 597-609.

Comas-Díaz, L. (in press). Integrative approach. In L. Comas-Díaz & B. Greene (Eds.), *Women of color and mental health.* New York: Guilford.

Comas-Díaz, L., & Jacobsen, F.M. (in press). Psychopharmacology for women of color: An empowerment approach. *Women & Therapy.*

Comas-Díaz, L., & Duncan, J.W. (1985). The cultural context: A factor in assertiveness training with mainland Puerto Rican women. *Psychology of Women Quarterly, 9,* 463-475.

de Beauvoir, S. (1961). *The second sex.* New York: Bantam Books.

Del Valle, M. (1989). *Acculturation, sex roles and racial definitions of Puerto Rican college students in Puerto Rico and the United States.* Dissertation presented at the Department of Education. Amherst: University of Massachusetts.

Espín, O.M. (1984, August). *Selection of Hispanic female healers in urban U.S. communities.* Paper presented at the annual meeting of the American Psychological Association, Toronto.

Franklin, A.J. & Boyd-Franklin, N. (1985). A psychoeducational perspective on Black parenting. In H. McAdoo & J. McAdoo (Eds.), *Black children.* Beverly Hills: Sage.

Ginorio, A.B. (1971). *A study of racial perception in Puerto Rico.* Unpublished master's thesis. Rio Piedras, Puerto Rico: Department of Psychology, University of Puerto Rico.

Gould, K.H. (1985). A minority-feminist perspective on child welfare issues. *Child Welfare, 64,* 291-305.

Greene, B. (1993). Human diversity in clinical psychology: Lesbians and gay sexual orientations. *The Clinical Psychologist, 46,* 74-82.

Greene, B. (1992). Still here: A perspective on psychotherapy with African American women. In J. Chrisler & D. Howard (Eds.), *New directions in feminist psychology: Practice, theory and research.* New York: Springer.

Greene, B. (1990). What has gone before: The legacy of racism and sexism in the lives of Black mothers and daughters. *Women & Therapy, 9,* 207-230.

Hall, C.I. (1992). Please choose one: The ethnic identity choices for biracial individuals. In M.P.P. Root (Ed.), *Racially mixed people in America*. Newbury Park: Sage Publications.

Hamilton, J.A. (1989). Emotional consequences of victimization and discrimination in "special populations" of women. In B. Parry (Ed.), *Women's disorders. Psychiatric Clinics of North America*. Philadelphia, PA: W.B. Saunders Co.

Hamilton, J.A., & Jensvold, M. (1992). Personality, psychopathology, and depressions in women. In L.S. Brown & M. Ballou (Eds.), *Personality and psychopathology: Feminist reappraisals*. New York: Guilford.

Helms, J.E. (Ed.) (1990). *Black and White racial identity: Theory, research and practice*. Westport, Connecticut: Greenwood Press.

Ho, M.H. (1987). *Family therapy with ethnic minorities*. Newbury Park, California: Sage.

Howard, G.S. (1991). Culture tales: A narrative approach to thinking, cross-cultural psychology, and psychotherapy. *American Psychologist, 46*, 187-197.

Jenkins, A. (1985). *Dialogue and dialectic: Psychotherapy in cross cultural contexts*. Presentation made at the American Psychological Association at the 93rd Annual Convention. Los Angeles.

Jorge, A. (1979) The black Puerto Rican woman in contemporary American society. In E. Acosta-Belén (Ed.), *The Puerto Rican woman*. New York: Praeger.

Kanuha, V. (1990). Compounding the triple jeopardy: Battering in lesbian of color relationships. *Therapy & Women, 9*, 169-184.

Koss-Chioino, J. (1992). *Women as healers, women as patients: Mental health care and traditional healing in Puerto Rico*. Boulder, CO: Westview Press.

Kovel, J. (1984). *White racism: A psychohistory*. New York: Columbia University Press.

Ladner, J. (1971). *Tomorrow's tomorrow: The Black woman*. Garden City, N.Y.: Doubleday.

Longres, J.F. (1974). Racism and its effects on Puerto Rican continentals. *Social Casework, 55*, 67-75.

Matsakis, A. (1992). *I can't get over it: A handbook for trauma survivors*. Oakland, CA: New Harbinger Publications, Inc.

Mays, V. & Comas-Díaz, L. (1988). Feminist therapies with ethnic minority populations: A closer look at Blacks and Hispanics. In M.A. Dutton-Douglas & L.E. Walker (Eds.), *Feminist psychotherapies: Integration of therapeutic and feminist systems*. New Jersey: Ablex Publishing Corp.

McGill, D.W. (1992). The cultural story in multicultural family therapy. *Families in Society, 73*, 339-349.

McGoldrick, M. & Gerson, R. (1985). *Genograms in family assessment*. New York: Norton.

Mizio, E. (1983). The impact of macro systems on Puerto Rican families. In G.J. Powell (Ed.), *The psychosocial development of minority group children*. New York: Brunner/Mazel.

Nakashira, C. (1992). An invisible monster: The creation and denial of mixed race people in America. In M.P.P. Root (Ed.), *Racially mixed people in America*. Newbury Park: Sage.

Nobles, W. (1980). Extended self: Rethinking the so-called Negro self-concept. In R.H. Jones (Ed.), *Black psychology*. New York: Harper & Row.

Oficina de Asuntos de la Mujer del Gobierno de Puerto Rico (1992, March 8). *La mujer puertorriqueña negra* (The Black Puerto Rican woman). Carolina, Puerto Rico: Colegio Universitario del Este.

Puig, A. (1991). A traumatic-stress model for EPAs. *EPA Digest, 12*, 22; 53-54.

Ramos Rosado, M. (1986). *La mujer puertorriqueña negra, "La otra cara de la historia" (The Black Puerto Rican woman, "The other face of history")*. *Homines, 10 (2)*, 491-497.

Rivera, E. (1982). *Family installments: Memories of growing up Hispanic*. New York: William Morrow & Co.

Root, M.P.P. (1990). Resolving the "other" status: Identity development of biracial individuals. *Women & Therapy, 9*, 185-205.

Root, M.P.P. (Ed.) (1992 a). *Racially mixed people in America*. Newbury Park, California: Sage.

Root, M.P.P. (1992 b). Reconstructing the impact of trauma on personality. In L.S. Brown & M. Ballou (Eds.), *Personality and psychopathology: Feminist reappraisals*. New York: Guilford Press.

Root, M.P.P. (in press). Mixed race women. In L. Comas-Díaz & B. Greene (Eds.), *Women of color and mental health*. New York: Guilford.

Seda Bonilla, E. (1970). *Requiem por una cultura*. (Requiem for a culture). Río Piedras, Puerto Rico: Editorial Edil.

Solomon, B.B. (1982). The delivery of mental health services to Afro-American individuals and families: Translating theory into practice. In B.A. Bass, G.J. Wyatt & G.J. Powell (Eds.), *The Afro-American family: Assessment, treatment and research issues*. New York: Grune & Stratton.

Thomas, P. (1967). *Down these mean streets*. New York: New American Library.

Vasquez, M. (in press). Latinas. In L. Comas-Díaz & B. Greene (Eds.), *Women of color and mental health*. New York: Guilford Press.

Walters, M., Carter, B., Papp, P., & Silverstein, O. (1988). *The invisible web: Gender patterns in family relationships*. New York: Guilford.

Zenón Cruz, I. (1975). *Narciso descubre su trasero* (Narcissus discovers his buttocks). Humacao, Puerto Rico: Editorial Furidi.

Social Inequalities
and Therapeutic Relationships:
Applying Freire's Ideas
to Clinical Practice

Eliana C. Korin

SUMMARY. Client-therapist differences related to culture, race, gender, and class are likely to create power imbalances and dilemmas in therapeutic relationships. It is argued that therapists' awareness of these social inequalities and participatory ideologies does not in itself necessarily eliminate the possibility of clinical impasses. Complex social and health realities[1] foster the perpetuation of an asymmetrical therapist-client relationship, creating contradictions in the helping process. To deal with this dilemma, a problem-posing method, based on Brazilian educator Paulo Freire's "Education for Critical Consciousness," is proposed. This method addresses the oppressive nature of non-reciprocal relationships, and involves both therapist and client/family in a process of mutual dialogue, conjoint reflection, and action.

The most interesting and inspiring problems are usually those that defy easy solutions. In clinical, teaching, and consulting practices the

Eliana C. Korin, Dipl. Psic., is a Faculty member at the Residency Program in Social Medicine/Department of Family Medicine, Albert Einstein College of Medicine. Address correspondence to the author at Department of Family Medicine, Montefiore Medical Center, 3544 Jerome Avenue, Bronx, NY 10467.

The author wishes to thank Rhea Almeida, editor, for her valuable suggestions and contributions to this essay.

[Haworth co-indexing entry note]: "Social Inequalities and Therapeutic Relationships: Applying Freire's Ideas to Clinical Practice." Korin, Eliana C. Co-published simultaneously in the *Journal of Feminist Family Therapy* (The Haworth Press, Inc.) Vol. 5, No. 3/4, 1994, pp. 75-98; and: *Expansions of Feminist Family Theory Through Diversity* (ed: Rhea V. Almeida) The Haworth Press, Inc., 1994, pp. 75-98. Multiple copies of this article/chapter may be purchased from The Haworth Document Delivery Center [1-800-3-HAWORTH; 9:00 a.m. - 5:00 p.m. (EST)].

most challenging situations often relate to problems that impede the helping process. These are the challenges that mobilize professional and personal growth.

A personal clinical dilemma that I encountered while working with Latina women in a public hospital in New York City led to many of the ideas generated in this paper. A number of years ago, already an experienced and culturally competent therapist, I started working with Puerto Rican, middle-aged women who had been referred for treatment mostly for symptoms of depression and anxiety. They usually responded well to my interventions, overcoming many of their original symptoms. Yet, I could not easily terminate treatment with a number of them, as new psychological or social needs repeatedly emerged, requiring my continued involvement. As a therapist, I became increasingly disempowered by feelings of frustration and helplessness. My clinical experience, in context with my own social and cultural realities, made me think that I might not be simply dealing with particular unresolved treatment issues. Instead, a social phenomenon manifested a clinical pattern, one that I came to identify as "chronic patienthood."[2] This clinical phenomenon–the clients' dependence–then, became redefined as a common life experience among those who live within a continuous cycle of oppression.

Isolation related to migration and fragmentation of family ties and the lack of natural support systems in the face of many social stresses were some of the important factors making these clients increasingly vulnerable to becoming dependent on the health care system for a continued source of support. And oppressive conditions present in the health care system–such as the tendency toward medicalization of problems, and discrimination in clinical practice– were also contributing to this process. I realized that, as a clinician, I had inadvertently become an agent for oppression by neglecting to make the examination of the complexities of the specific social context influencing my clients' lives a central focus of the therapeutic process.

But of what use was this insight to me? It was an important realization, but I still had a dilemma. The clients expected *me* to help them. How could I address the social problem clinically? How could I avoid perpetuating the problem with solutions at the wrong level? Also, how could I help them to become more independent and in charge of their lives, without reinforcing their passivity with *my* too active efforts to help them?

It was my struggle with these questions that led me to turn to the ideas of Paulo Freire, a Brazilian educator whose method had helped me before when I was working with poor, black parents in Brazil. Freire's problem-posing method interweaves personal and social realities in order to promote critical consciousness through analysis of the dynamics of the oppressor-oppressed. These ideas inspired me to new ways of thinking and working with these poor, Puerto Rican, middle-aged women in New York City.

In this paper, I will present some ideas about how both to avoid and deal with these clinical impasses, using Freire's approach. My focus will be on the ways in which the larger context of social inequalities contributes to an imbalance of power in therapeutic relationships.

ISSUES OF POWER IN FAMILY THERAPY

Major changes have occurred in the family therapy field since feminist therapists (Hare-Mustin, 1978; Goldner, 1985; Walters, Carter, Papp, and Silverstein, 1988; McGoldrick, Anderson and Walsh, 1989; Luepnitz, 1988) introduced power as a central and controversial theme in family discourse, and proposed an analysis of the family based on social and cultural realities. Until recently, most of the feminist critique in family therapy has been focused primarily on the politics of gender; less attention has been paid to the impact of race, culture, and class on family relations. Although the main focus in feminist therapy has been on the experience of white middle-class women in relation to male oppression, some feminists have addressed and validated in their writings the unique experiences of women of color (Luepnitz, 1988; Goodrich et al., 1988).

Historically, feminists have invited the discussion of oppression in families, but only a few have expanded this scholarship to include the dimensions of culture, race, class as well as gender (Imber-Black, 1988, 1990; Pinderhughes, 1989; McGoldrick, 1982). We have yet to develop a systematic analysis of the interaction between those dimensions and family dynamics (Kleiman, in press).

Moreover, feminists in family therapy have paid less attention to consideration of the social and cultural inequities that affect therapeutic relationships and the helping context. A few notable exceptions are Mustin's (1978) references to the need of a contractual approach to allow family control of the therapeutic process; the contribution of Aponte's (1985) work on the therapist's own values; and Imber-Black's (1988) thorough analysis of the impact of larger systems on women and families.

More recently, some family therapists (White, 1990; Flaskas and Humphreys, 1993) have suggested the usefulness of the French philosopher Foucault's ideas on knowledge and power in revising Bateson's (1972) controversial notions of power: power as circular, therefore never unilateral; and, power as toxic, therefore to be excluded in family therapy. White has applied Foucault's ideas in his work with Epston (1990) on helping clients to re-author their life stories. Interestingly, while he applies Foucault's ideas to suggest that therapists critically examine the use of therapeutic practices regarding power, he does not include a consideration of the social and cultural realities of his clients' lives.

As Fisch critiques this interpretation of Foucault (1993), he says:

> Regrettably what White and Epston's (1990) selective use of Foucault and de Shazer's (1991) reliance on de Man-style deconstruction have in common is that they reinforce tendencies, already present in Batesonian and constructivist-based therapies, to conceptually isolate the therapist-family system from any social, historical, economic, or institutional context, and to deny the existence or relevance of differences in power at an interpersonal level. (p. 6)

The trend in family therapy is to embrace the narrative approach unequivocally, while retaining some elements of constructivism. This leads to a focus on narratives, and on the analysis of cultural meanings and beliefs within a personal story. Further, the therapeutic task has been redefined as a conversation (Anderson & Goolishian, 1990; Hoffman, 1990), changing the role of the therapist to become less directive and hierarchical, less that of an expert.

Many feminist therapists have incorporated a constructivist approach into their clinical work (Hare-Mustin, 1989, 1991; Goldner,

1988; Hoffman, 1990, 1992; Allen and Laird, 1990; Weigarten, 1991; Sheinberg, 1992). This focus on personal narratives, and the utilization of methods such as text deconstruction, has important limitations, however, because it overemphasizes the personal at the expense of obscuring multiple social contexts that are oppressive to the individual.

In this same article Fisch quotes Waldegrave (1990) as saying:

> Constructivist approaches to family therapy can fall into the same trap as the systemic approach. The realities created by both family members and therapists are viewed as interpretive observer descriptions, each carrying their own meaning. The denial of objective reality in these observer descriptions can lead therapists to treat the attributions of meaning given by different family members as being of equal value. The stories of abused children and women . . . are more likely to reflect what really happens in a household, than the reduced story a person who abuses often gives. (p. 31)

Concerned with inequalities dictated by differences of social power, feminists have been alert to the limiting aspects of a narrative perspective that is uncritical of the larger sociopolitical context. Laird (1989), proposing the use of the therapy-story to legitimize and include women's stories as part of the social discourse, says:

> In family therapy we tend, in general, to be more interested in the particular narratives and stories of individuals and families, rather than the sociocultural narratives that construct the contextual realms of possibility from which individuals and families can select the ingredients and focus for their own narratives. (p. 430)

Freire's ideas and method are especially relevant to bridging these two realms because they validate both the importance of cultural meanings and the existence of a social reality. He states,

> Although the dialectical relations of men [women] with the world exist independently of how these relations are perceived (or whether or not they are perceived at all), it is also

true that the form of action men [women] adopt is to a large extent a function of how they perceive themselves in the world. (Freire, 1982, p. 71)

One cannot conceive of objectivity without subjectivity. Neither one can exist without the other, nor can they be dichotomized. (Freire, 1982, p. 35)

SOCIAL DETERMINANTS OF THERAPEUTIC DILEMMAS

An examination of clients' social realities requires the understanding of the impact of social inequalities upon their lives. This implies the following premises:

- Social inequalities dictated by gender, race, class, and culture have a direct impact on health and psychological status and influence the way people seek and receive treatment. For instance, research findings have indicated that poverty and minority status are related to feelings of powerlessness, helplessness, and social isolation, affecting mortality and morbidity rates (Syme, 1976, 1986; U.S. DHHS Secretary Task Force, 1985; Gaventa, 1980).
- Illness or psychological symptoms can be a response to the lack of power and control or to a sense of helplessness in the face of oppressive living conditions. In some circumstances, depression, for instance, can be understood as a manifestation of lack of power and demoralization instead of a pathological event, or both (James and McIntyre, 1983; Pinderhughes, 1989).
- Individuals and families have unequal social power depending upon their social and economic status (Inclan and Ferran, 1990), which affects the dynamics of therapeutic relations and individual and family function.
- Both clients and clinicians are often disempowered by a system that, given its organization and predominant ideologies, fosters the perpetuation of a therapist-client relationship in which the clinician is defined as the competent-giver, and the client as the helpless, incompetent-recipient of care.[3]

What are the implications of these premises for clinical practice? Clinical problems need to be contextualized in social terms. In other words, the definition of the client/family's problem has to include a consideration of oppressive realities related to the larger social context. Second, the therapeutic relationship has to be re-framed in non-hierarchical terms by the therapist demystifying his/her authority/knowledge and by recognizing the client/family's competencies and life expertise. And finally, the client and the therapist have to be engaged in a dialogue to co-investigate a particular social context that affects the client/family's lives as well as the therapeutic process.

Let us return to the story relating to my dilemma with my Puerto Rican clients in order to illustrate the ways in which I have incorporated these premises into my practice.

Once I could redefine the problem–the clients' dependence–within a social frame, I came to terms with my feelings of frustration. I decided then to share the therapeutic dilemma with my clients, inviting them to reflect jointly on the problem I had articulated: that is, the more successful I was in helping them to feel better, the more dependent they were on my continued help.[4] I proceeded by sharing that this was also a dilemma occurring with other Puerto Rican middle-aged clients, and that this had made me think that the dilemma was related to common stresses they all might be experiencing. I then added that I had realized I needed their help in identifying and examining these stresses to be more helpful to them. That is, I needed to learn with and from them some things they knew and I did not. My concern, in relating my dilemma then, was not simply of a technical order, nor was my intention a strategic move. It involved a true invitation to my clients to take a critical position vis-à-vis both myself the therapist, the helping structures, and, inevitably, the larger society as well. An important element in the dialogue, at this point, was my sincere belief that my clients had a knowledge that I did not have. In other words, they were capable knowers in spite of their passivity, and they could become my teachers.

This process evolved as a co-investigation, or unveiling, of their lives and clinical problems in relation to the oppressive aspects of their experience as "patients," as middle-aged women of color, as first-generation Puerto Rican/New Yorkers, etc. I asked them to focus on their psychological stresses, relating them to their social status (race, cultural minority, class, gender, age), and also to comment on their experiences with professionals as well as the health care and human services systems. In other words, my clients and I together examined both the therapeutic dilemma and the clinical problems in relation to specific conditions of oppression present in their lives. We became involved in a process of consciousness-raising that included both the recognition and analysis of oppression related to culture, race, class, as well as gender and age, and the understanding of its implication to the helping process. Thus, we connected personal issues and social themes, thereby fostering a new understanding of the problems as well as new ideas on how to address them.[5]

It is important to note here that even though my cultural and gender identification with these clients helped me with the formation of the therapeutic alliance, it did not eliminate the possibility of a clinical impasse. Cultural identification or sensitivity and sociopolitical awareness are important, but they do not necessarily free the professional from misunderstanding clients and families (Comas-Díaz, 1991). As we become assimilated to and educated by the dominant culture and its institutions, we are likely to absorb its values uncritically. As experts, we become prescribers or guardians of an established social order. On the other hand, differences in culture, race, gender, class, and often age and sexual identity, when unexamined, are likely to compound imbalances of power/asymmetries of power in the clinical relationship. Other factors that possibly contribute to clinical misunderstandings relate to the personal dimensions of the therapist. Certainly the therapist's personal stories, interpersonal style, attitudes, as well as her/his beliefs and values, are most influential in the dynamics of the therapeutic relationship.

Many clinical impasses occur when the therapist ignores fundamental differences of values and beliefs in his/her interaction with clients. By being aware of these possible differences, and exploring the client's/family's values and beliefs, he/she often facilitates the therapeutic alliance and prevents difficulties in treatment. The therapist has to validate the client's/family's experiences explicitly and address differences of values directly or indirectly.

Both an ethnographic perspective (Kleinman et al., 1978; Like and Steiner, 1988) and culture-oriented circular questioning (Mauksch & Roesler, 1990) have been suggested as useful approaches to guide clinicians in eliciting a family's belief systems. However, the simple understanding or identification of differences of meaning is insufficient to avoid impasses when power asymmetries between client and therapist (related to class, race, etc.) are present. Again, I emphasize the importance of the influence of culture, race and class–as well as of gender, age, and sexual orientation–on the attitudes, values, and beliefs (Karrer, 1988) that ultimately determine the balances of power in the clinical relationship. The pendulum of power between client/family and therapist will swing differently depending on the social status of the participants in various contexts. For instance: the situation of a white, middle-class, woman therapist treating an African-American, working-class family will produce different constraints from a situation where an African-American woman therapist, from a working-class background, is treating a white, middle-class family (Boyd-Franklin, 1989). The situation will also be different depending upon where treatment takes place; in a private office or in a public hospital, in a racially integrated community or in a segregated one. It is important that these social diversities of inequality and differences be consciously addressed by the therapist as he/she engages the client in a process of mutual learning about his/her cultural beliefs. Also, this process must lead the therapist to re-evaluate his/her own presuppositions or preconcepts (Santamaria, 1990) about the client's cultural values or beliefs.

The following clinical situation from my private practice illustrates some of these points:

Case I: Aiming for the Best

Joan, a 38-year-old, African American Jehovah's Witness, who worked as a clerk and lived in the South Bronx, came for therapy to deal with anxiety attacks. She was also interested in discussing stresses related to past and present negative behaviors, as she defined them, of family members. As a middle-class, non-religious Latina, I asked myself: "What are my preconceptions about this client as an African American woman living in the South Bronx, as a Jehovah's witness, etc.? or about her family, especially considering 'negative behaviors'? What are the implications of our differences in race, socioeconomic status, educational and religious beliefs?"

I acknowledged and integrated these differences in the therapeutic dialogue. For instance, considering her socioeconomic situation, I was ready to accept only a symbolic fee, but avoiding an asymmetrical decision-making process or a paternalistic approach, I decided first to explore her own ideas of how the treatment should be. After listening to some of her stories relating why she came for treatment, I chose to focus on the social class issues, and on the socioeconomic aspects of her choice of therapist, to acknowledge and explore issues related to social mobility, and to introduce an examination of class differences relevant to the therapeutic relationship. I asked her: "You are not the typical client who seeks out a private therapist. Usually people with your economic and living situation are more likely to seek help at an agency or public hospital. Yet, in spite of the odds, you decided to find a private therapist and succeeded in getting one. How did you go about this choice? How did you decide you wanted a private therapist?"

With her unassuming manner, this fashionably dressed woman explained how, in spite of her poor background and current income level, she always aimed for the best. (She was an expert in used clothes stores, and she had exceptional sewing skills.) Her answers indicated she was hoping for a lower fee but not too low, and definitely not for a waiver. She was prepared to explore the possibility of a reduced number of sessions–that is, to work with what was possible, even if that meant I had to change my preferred approach to the problem.

Later in the therapeutic process I also asked her: "What do you think would be the advantages/disadvantages and risks and gains of having a therapist from a different cultural and social backgrounds, who is not black, who has not lived in a poor neighborhood, who is not a Jehovah's Witness, etc.?" She was somewhat surprised with these questions and responded by giving little importance to our differences then. Some time after, she talked about her brother–the only other sibling financially and emotionally independent–criticizing his animosity against whites as anti-Christian and antisocial. On the one hand, she was confirming the relevance of integrating racial issues in our dialogue; on the other, she was also expressing a naive (versus critical) consciousness[6] regarding race, which needed to be challenged especially by a non-black therapist.

Recognizing my own preconceptions regarding her religious beliefs, I also asked her: "I don't know enough of your religion, and maybe what I know is wrong. Please tell me how your idea of coming for therapy is understood by your elders (religious leaders) or your congregation?" To my surprise, the decision to come to therapy, and others of her choices, were not in conflict with her religion, as I first thought. My work with her not only changed my views about Jehovah's Witnesses somewhat and my ideas about "typical" private practice clients, but also helped me, once more, to re-examine my own race and class issues.

The therapist's capacity for self-critique and self-awareness are definitely basic elements in the therapeutic process. But it is important that a self-examination also include the social dimension of the therapist's self (cultural, class, race, background), not just the personal dimension. Too often clinicians unwittingly invite clients to play the dependent role by fully ignoring clients' everyday experiences and life expertise, and limiting their active participation in treatment. This is more likely to occur when social inequities of race, class, and culture operate without acknowledgement within the therapeutic relationship. Usually this process occurs in a benevolent manner, when a therapist attempts to help by either patronizing or rescuing his/her client, or when efforts to educate turn into "sermons." Let us consider, for instance, the following situation:

Case II: A "Grateful" Wife

Ana, a Latina, working-class woman, told her therapist that she was having her fourth abortion in a period of two years. The therapist was struck by the client's passivity regarding her husband's reluctance to use birth control. All attempts to engage her husband in sessions had been unsuccessful. The therapist, an experienced white feminist, from an Anglo-Saxon background, found herself caught in a negative complementary relationship with this client, and becoming increasingly active in sessions in the face of the client's passivity. She was uncomfortable with her tendency to "prescribe" behavior to the client.

The therapeutic dilemma was: How does the therapist prevent her/his knowledge from becoming "pedagogical" and the client's knowledge from becoming further "oppressed?" The therapist's social consciousness and her collaborative-oriented ideology in clinical work helped her to recognize the clinical impasse and seek a consultation with me. An awareness of the impact of her class, race, and cultural status on the treatment, and an emphasis on social inequalities in the therapeutic relationship, allowed a repositioning of herself, which further mobilized Ana, the client, toward action. This was possible when I guided the therapist to recognize the central importance of acknowledging differences of social privilege (related to race and class status) between them and of exploring the life realities of this client in relation to changing cultural and social contexts. She learned that Ana, an immigrant from Peru of indigenous heritage, was able to dramatically change her social status from poverty to working-class standards by immigrating to United States and by marrying her husband, a Peruvian of European background, a good provider, and a hardworking man. When the therapist understood Ana's behavior as a gesture of gratitude versus simple subservience toward her husband, it became easier for her to help this client toward self-affirmation both in the therapeutic relationship and in the family.

The client became more active, able to articulate her story, only after the therapist recognized and validated the client's life experiences in a larger social context. This complex case illustrates the importance, and also the challenge, of integrating an interactive analysis of race, culture, class, and gender to clinical problems.

The complexity of the social problems, each with their own origins of oppression, presented by clients—isolation, neglect, fragmentation of social ties, alienation—create a context of inequality within which help is sought. These are not easily solvable problems. The interplay of social differences in therapeutic relationships creates subtle traps in the helping process, which disempowers both clients and clinicians. Even a socially minded family therapist will still struggle with the dilemma of how to address patients' problematic behaviors such as passivity, helplessness, and inappropriate expectations without creating an asymmetrical client-therapist relationship.

As therapists, how do we avoid negative attitudes, such as those described above, that ultimately defeat therapeutic attempts? And finally, how do we address the inevitable interplay of power differentials in therapeutic relationships when social inequalities created by class, gender, race, or culture (and sometimes sexual orientation, age, and disability) are present? In other words, how do we avoid creating therapeutic relationships that ultimately perpetuate the same oppressive order we want to change in the client's social context?

Recognizing both the complexity involved in the therapeutic task and the social realities that define the helping context, I am suggesting the relevance of Freire's method to guide clinicians in addressing these problematic clinical and social realities, while attending to the imbalance of power within therapeutic relationships.

I am proposing a model of empowerment that involves both individual *and* social empowerment. From this perspective, empowerment is defined as "a process in which people develop a greater sense of self-worth and self-confidence," but *also* "a process in which people understand how the broader social world has defined their lives and realize the potential they have for more actively influencing their own environment" (Rappaport, 1984). Following Freire's method, client and therapist become involved in a process of mutual learning, dialogue, and conjoint reflection, which ultimately empowers and liberates both client and clinician.

WHAT IS EDUCATION FOR CRITICAL CONSCIOUSNESS?

In his book "Pedagogy of the Oppressed" (Freire, 1982), Freire explains how the traditional model of education is an instrument of oppression and serves to reinforce social inequities. He says knowledge is used as a tool for oppression rather than an experience to share. He analyses the contradictions[7] involved in the learner-teacher relationship, defined as one of oppressed-oppressor, and he proposes a "problem-posing" approach in which learning is a mutual process, involving critical thinking. Learner and teacher, in a process of conjoint reflection, pose problems and work together to transform an oppressive reality. This method–"Education for Critical Consciousness"–involves a *dialogical* approach to change, requires critical *reflection,* and promotes readiness toward *action.*

Empowerment involves the development of a critical consciousness, the level of consciousness in which the individual becomes aware of being creator and owner of his/her own destiny. The individual becomes empowered by a new sense of selfhood and often takes the initiative toward changing social structures around him/her. In other words, he/she becomes subject, not object of his/her own experience. Freire's ideas, when translated to clinical practice, suggest a similar process.

For instance, Joan (my client aiming for the best), was, in spite of her social achievements, still living in a very poor neighborhood in a building now in decay. She told me:

> I have been thinking, I am black, I am a woman, and I can't move out of that building. But there is something I can do: I can talk to other neighbors who want the same thing I do and force the landlord and the police to clean up the building. I feel better, to make *them* worry about it, not me.

This client's promptness in acting to attempt to change a particular oppressive reality (housing) around her was preceded by many sessions in which she shared her experiences (dialogue) of disenfranchisement. These stories were examined (reflection) both in relation to her family relations as well as to the larger social context of her life. These were stories of poverty–her father's economic disenfranchisement–and racial discrimination. While listening to her stories of growing up, I questioned her about the experience of living in Harlem, contrasted with the Harlem of today, and also, with her experiences moving to the Bronx. My questions addressed housing availability, rent issues, neighborhood composition, etc., focusing on housing in relation to racial and economic factors. My intent was to help her to organize the facts and experiences, and then to formulate their related problems, within a sociohistorical frame expanding from a psychological one. It is interesting to note that I did not remember referring specifically to issues of discrimination; at this stage of treatment, I had not shared my views or my values with her. Yet, her disposition for action at this stage indicated that she had moved to a different level of consciousness–critical consciousness–which mobilized her to action.

EDUCATION FOR CRITICAL CONSCIOUSNESS IN CLINICAL PRACTICE

Freire offers us a method for questioning the nature of the therapist-client relationship, which is especially helpful in either avoiding or dealing with therapeutic impasses. An important element distinguishing this approach is the elimination of the asymmetrical, often paternalistic role of the therapist in clinical relationships. Within this approach the therapist's goals are to demystify knowledge, eliminate arguments based on authority, and generate a redefinition of hierarchies of power in clinical relationships, allowing the client to be active and exercise control of the process. This framing of the therapeutic relationship can only occur when the therapist acknowledges the impact of social inequalities in the therapeutic relationship. From a Freirian perspective, the therapeutic task also involves a process of social critique. Families are coached to discover themselves in relationship to their social world, to view personal problems in relation to a larger context, and to see themselves beyond their problems, not circumscribed by them.

Dialogue

When translated to clinical practice, this method promotes dialogue between client and therapist, in which the therapist listens to the client/family stories and asks them about their life experiences as they relate to their personal problems and a particular social context. The process has some similarities to a narrative approach (White and Epston, 1990; Laird, 1989), but differs from it by including a direct inquiry into larger social determinants (race, class, culture, as well as gender). The therapist's systematic questioning addresses the specific social context in which clients' experiences are embedded, in order to identify sources of oppression and then to examine critically the impact of that oppression on the client/family's views.

This dialogue is moved by curiosity, interest, and empathy, guided by a basic belief in people's capacity to provide insights about themselves and the world surrounding them. In this regard, the development of the therapist's attitudes regarding race, class, and culture is as important as the sharpening of her/his skills as a listener and a problem-poser.

At an initial stage, questions should be descriptive, focusing on manifestations of the problem in its social, historical, and relational context. This technique of questioning is similar to the systemic, circular question (Penn, 1985; Tomm, 1987, 1988), but expands categories to include relationships within a larger sociopolitical context. The questions I ask reveal the complexities of my clients' lives, weaving in and out of social and personal realms: some supportive and others oppressive. In the case of Ana, I listened to her experiences while considering her condition of being an immigrant, of being Latina, of being an indigenous person, coming from a poor background and ascending to the working class. When interviewing her as a consultant I inquired: "What would women in your native country say about your problem with your husband?" She answered: "They would say I should do what my husband says because he is good to me, he gives me things. . . ." "Do other immigrant women from your country and living here see this situation as you see it?" "I don't know; some women, when they move here they change with their husbands, sometimes their husbands leave them and they don't have money. . . ." After some questions and discussion related to why these women, and their husbands, changed, she was able to articulate her own needs and desire for change, which had been suppressed by her fear that her husband would leave her and that she would lose his economic support. I followed this with questions focused on the economic aspects of the problem, such as: "How is your life here in United States compared to life in your country of origin, in relation to money, housing, etc.?" With enthusiasm, she described how comfortable her life here was compared to the conditions of social deprivation in which she had lived in Peru. As the treatment processed, this client was able to feel more empowered to express her needs and desires to her husband, finally negotiating with him the use of contraceptives.

A new dialogue with her husband emerged from the new dialogue with me as consultant and with her therapist. And her therapist's social consciousness evolved as she recognized the importance of including class, race, and culture as determinants equally relevant as gender in the therapeutic process.

In a problem-posing method, questions are guided both by clinical parameters and a social analysis. In contrast to Milan systemic therapists (Palazolli et al., 1980), Freire's premise is that no helping relationship is value-neutral. The person of the therapist, her/his life history and social background will determine the terms of the relationship. Therefore, a self-awareness in relation to clients' social background is crucial for orienting therapists' questions or statements. Validation of the family's experience and reference to their strengths–the therapist feedback–are also critical to facilitate dialogue and to promote client empowerment. This process should also lead to the identification and validation of client/family resources through therapists' statements and interpretations of their experiences.

A genogram is a useful tool to complement this process, considering intergenerational dynamics as they relate to a sociohistorical context. The idea is for both therapist and client/family to be involved in a process of *co-investigation* of the personal and social realities that surround the client/family's life, a process in which the family members will also teach the therapist. Central themes are identified ("meaningful thematics") by both client and therapist, relating both to a relational and sociopolitical context. In the case of Joan, my client who aimed for the best, her anxiety attacks, one of her presenting problems, were related to conflicts between her loyalty to her family and her personal aspirations, as well as to the experience of discrimination she felt daily in contact with multiple social institutions.

Reflection

Such dialogue evolves into a process of conjoint reflection. "The goal of the dialogue is critical thinking or posing problems, in such a way to uncover the root causes–economic, political, psychological, cultural, historical–for the [family] client's problems" (Wallerstein, 1988).

Questions focused on "how" (relational questions) and "why" questions (related to the root causes of the problem) are instrumental in promoting critical thinking. The therapist uses "how" questions to help clients to relate facts, experiences, and realities, to identify patterns among them, and, finally, to conceptualize themes ("generative themes," using Freirian terminology). For instance, while listening to Joan's report on a particular experience, I would ask her: "*How* does this experience relate to the fact that you are African American? *How* is your experience as an African American different from other black women? other minorities (race)? *How* does the fact that you are a woman (gender) and that you are well-educated (class) have an impact on you?" Some themes identified through these sequences of questions were issues of racism (related to her and her family/friends' repeated experiences of discrimination), instability of class status among blacks (related to experiences of employment changes among brother and church friends), and the stereotyping of black women (related to some of her own and her friends' experiences with male friends and employers). Questions involving comparisons or contrasts of experiences, time, and location are helpful to guide clients into different levels of reflection and to facilitate an understanding of problems from a social perspective. For instance, I asked Joan: "*How* is your situation different from other women? Different from your mother, from your niece?" Through these questions, Joan could understand the differences of social opportunity between her, her mother, and her niece within a sociohistorical framework.

"Why" questions address root causes of problems, promoting a social analysis of a particular experience. For instance, I asked Joan, regarding her father's beatings of her mother: "*Why* do you think he did that?" "Because he was drunk." "*Why* was he drunk?" "Because of frustrations at work." "Not all alcoholic men beat their wives, *why* might he have done so?" "Because he had a bad temper." After some discussion about men's violent behaviors, male socialization, alcoholism, I continued my inquiry: "What triggers his bad temper?" "His frustrations of being undervalued at work, etc." Joan then focused on her father's job situation, expanding her analysis to examine critically the experiences of African American males in relation to work, family, and other social institutions. Given the fact that all social determinants (race/gender/class/culture) have equal weight, the challenge in the therapeutic encounter becomes how to choose the order in which to integrate these determinants into the questions the therapist asks. In other words, the focus of the questions is not arbitrary; it is determined by the nature of the problem and by the clients' particular social reality.

Contradictions are identified, problems are redefined, unfolding new perspectives for client/family and therapist. My client, Joan had described her father as both a good provider and caring father, as well as a violent husband. I coached Joan into reflecting on these two realities with my questions related to race and socioeconomic factors, together with gender socialization. Joan then reinterpreted what she had presented as her mother's "weakness" as the self-sacrifice of an educated woman who felt she had to match the feelings of her husband (from a poor background) regarding his powerlessness vis-à-vis underemployment. Joan's evolving views on women's role in our society seemed to conflict with her apparent acceptance of the exclusion of women from some decision-making tasks in her church. When I presented her with these contradictions, she reflected on them. She ended up elaborating on the need of her church to review its organizational structure and include women in more central roles.

Action

The last aspect of Freire's process of "conscientization" is action. Client/families are mobilized to initiate action to change their context. A most important aspect of Freire's education for critical consciousness is facilitating people's actions toward transforming their lives, challenging what he calls "limit situations" (e.g., disability, unemployment, etc.). Critical thinking allows people to be able to relate but also to differentiate individual from social problems; therefore, the elimination of self-blame must also involve taking personal responsibility for individual and social change.

Let us contrast the situation of two women suffering from anxiety attacks: one, my client, Joan tended to blame herself for handling some oppressive social situations poorly. Her approach contrasted with another African-American client, a community leader, who tended to use her political consciousness to avoid examination of painful, personal, and family realities. At times her political and community activities shielded her from dealing with conflicts with dependent family members, who often created conditions that exacerbated her anxiety. In both cases, a validation of social oppression was an important aspect of their therapy. For Joan, the treatment had to promote a process of reflection in order to mobilize social consciousness and, therefore, social action. The focus of my treatment with my community leader client was to help her to reflect on the personal dimensions of her life. According to Freire, there is no merit to personal change when it is divorced from change at the social level; there is no legitimacy to social action without a corresponding concern with personal issues.

CONCLUSION

The feminist critique has enriched the family therapy discourse in recent years by addressing issues of power/control within family life and emphasizing these dynamics in the therapeutic process. In this paper I have suggested that clinical dilemmas are likely to occur when differences of power related to race, culture, and class differences between client and therapist are not identified and addressed in therapy. My experience with Paulo Freire's method indicates that his ideas can be very instrumental in clinical practice to guide the therapist in a process of self and social analysis related to social inequalities affecting both the therapeutic process and clients' lives. His method—education for critical consciousness—empowers both client and therapist to deal with the contradictions presented in the helping process and to promote change at a personal and social level.

Freire's method has not been so successful with groups who lack a sense of community. Therefore, connecting clients and families is essential. Critical consciousness cannot be promoted without a basic sense of connection among people. In this regard, family therapy within a larger systems framework has a lot to offer because of its focus on building and strengthening relationships among people. On the other hand, Freire's approach offers a unique contribution to family therapy, expanding its scope to address power differentials in therapeutic relationships and the social dimensions of clients'/families' problems more effectively.

NOTES

1. The term "health realities" is used here to refer to many realities or aspects regarding clients' experience with health issues: the dynamics of the health care system and the client-clinician relationship; clients' health attitudes and behaviors; patterns of help-seeking behaviors; issues related to their mental health status, etc.

2. Other authors, such as Talcott Parsons (1958), David Mechanic (1961), Irving Zola (1966), and Stephen Cole (1972) have discussed this problem from a sociological point of view in describing the "sick role." Lazare (1975) coined the term "patienthood" to focus on client/clinician relationships in mental health settings from a consumer perspective. I use the term "chronic patienthood" here to highlight the ways in which the issues of chronicity and dependence influence the dynamics of therapeutic relationships.

3. The language in medical systems is revealing in this respect; we say "mental health provider" and "patient."

4. This inquiry initially took place in individual or family interviews. Later, we continued the dialogue in group sessions with the clients involved.

5. In collaboration with some of these clients, I developed a community participatory program for Latina women, involving activation of a support network and including a health education and an empowerment perspective. This program has been active for twelve years. Currently, two of the leaders of this program are from the original pool of clients cited in my story.

6. Freire defines three levels of social consciousness: naive, mythological, and critical consciousness. Naive and mythological are both less developed stages and involve distortions. A naive conscious person accepts his/her oppressed role as a given, and is fatalistic about this role. The mythological conscious person recognizes oppression, but acts guided more by his/her emotions than reason (Freire, 1973). The concept of critical consciousness will be described later in this paper.

7. The term "contradictions" here refers to the dialectical conflict between opposing social forces (Freire, 1973).

REFERENCES

Andersen, T. (1987). The reflecting team: Dialogue and metadialogue in clinical work. *Family Process*, 26, 415-428.

Anderson, H. & Goolishian, H.A. (1990). Beyond cybernetics: Comments on Atkinson and Heath's: "Further thoughts on second order family therapy." *Family Process*, 29, 157-163.

Aponte, H.J. (1985). The negotiation of value in family therapy. *Family Process*, 24, 323-338.

Bateson, G. (1972). *Steps to an ecology of mind.* New York: Ballantine Books.

Bograd, M. (1984). Family systems approaches to wife battering: A feminist critique. *American Journal of Orthopsychiatry*, 54, 558-568.

Boyd-Franklin, N. (1989). *Black families in therapy: A multi-system approach.* New York: Guilford Press.

Cole, S. and Lejeune, R. (1972). Illness and legitimation of failure. *American Sociological Review,* 37, 347-356.

Comas-Díaz, L. & Jacobsen, F.M. (1991). Ethnocultural transference and counter-transference in the therapeutic dyad. *American Journal of Orthopsychiatry,* 6, 392-402.

Fisch, V. (1993). Poststructuralism in family therapy: Interrogating the narrative/conversational mode. *Journal of Marital and Family Therapy,* 19, 221-232.

Flaskas, C. & Humphreys, C. (1993). Theorizing about power: Intersecting ideas of Foucault with the "problem" of power in family therapy. *Family Process,* 32, 35-46.

Freire, P. (1973). *Education for critical consciousness.* New York: Continuum.

Freire, P. (1982). *Pedagogy of the oppressed.* New York: Continuum.

Gaventa, J. (1980). *Power and powerlessness.* Chicago, University of Illinois Press.

Goldner, V. (1985). Feminism and family therapy. *Family Process* 24, 31-48.

Goldner, V. (1988). Generation and gender: Normative and covert hierarchies. *Family Process,* 27, 17-31.

Goodrich, T.J., Rampage, C., Ellman, B. & Halstead, K. (1988). *Feminist family therapy: A casebook.* New York: W.W. Norton.

Hare-Mustin, R.T. (1978). A feminist approach to family therapy. *Family Process,* 17, 181-194.

Hare-Mustin, R.T. (1989). The problem of gender in family therapy theory (pp. 61-77). In M. McGoldrick, C. Anderson, F. Walsh (Eds.), *Women in families.* New York: W.W. Norton.

Hare-Mustin, R.T. (1991). Sex, lies and headaches: The problem is power, (pp. 63-86). In T.J. Goodrich (Ed.), *Women and power.* New York: W.W. Norton.

Hoffman, L. (1990). Constructing realities: An art of lenses. *Family Process,* 29, 1-12.

Hoffman, L. (1992). A reflexive stance for family therapy, (pp. 7-25). In S. McNamee and D. Gergen (Eds.), *Therapy as social construction.* Newbury Park, CA: Sage Publications.

Imber-Black, E. (1988). *Families and larger systems.* The Guilford Press.

Imber-Black, E. (1990). Multiple embedded systems (pp. 3-18). In M. P. Mirkin (Ed.), The social and political contexts of family therapy. Boston: Allyn and Bacon.

Inclan, J. and Ferran, E. (1990). Poverty, politics and family therapy: A role for systems theory (pp. 193-213). In M. P. Mirkin (Ed.), *The social and political contexts of family therapy.* Boston: Allyn and Bacon.

James, K. & McIntyre, D. (1983). The reproduction of families: The social role of family therapy. *Journal of Marital Family Therapy,* 9, 119-129.

Karrer, B. (1988). The sound of the hands clapping (pp. 209-237). In G. Saba, K. Hardy, & B. Karrer. (Eds.), *Minorities and family therapy.* NY: The Haworth Press, Inc.

Kleinman, A., Eisenberg, L. & Good, B. (1978). Culture, illness and care: Clinical lessons from anthropologic and cross cultural research. *Annals of Internal Medicine,* 88, 251-258.

Kliman, J. (in press). The interweaving of gender, class and race in family therapy. In M. P. Mirkin (Ed.), *Reweaving the tapestry: A feminist reconstruction of women and psychotherapy.* New York: The Guilford Press.

Laird, J. (1989). Women and stories: Restorying women's self-construction. (pp. 427-450). In M. McGoldrick, C.H. Anderson, & F. Walsh (Eds.), *Women in families.* New York: W.W. Norton.

Lazare, A., Einsenthal, S. & Wasserman, L. (1975). The customer approach to patienthood. *Archives General Psychiatry* 32, 553-558.

Like, R.C., & Steiner, P. (1986). Medical anthropology and the family physician. *Family Medicine,* 19, 87-92.

Luepnitz, D. (1988). *The family interpreted: Feminist theory in clinical practice.* New York: Basic Books.

Mauksch, L.B. & Roesler, T. (1990). Expanding the context of the patient's explanatory model using circular questioning. *Family Systems Medicine,* 8, 3-13.

McGoldrick, M., Pearce, J.K. & Giordano, J. (Eds.) (1982). *Ethnicity and family therapy.* New York: The Guilford Press.

McGoldrick, M., Anderson, C. & Walsh, E. (Eds.) (1989). *Women in families: A framework for family therapy.* New York: W.W. Norton.

Mechanic, D. and Volkhart, E. (1961). Stress, illness behavior and the sick role. *American Sociological Review,* 26, 51-58.

Parsons, T. (1958). Definitions of health and illness in the light of American values and social structure (pp. 165-187). In E. Gartly Jaco (Ed.), *Patients, physicians and illness.* Glencoe, Illinois: The Free Press.

Penn, P. (1985). Circular questioning. *Family Process,* 24, 299-310.

Pinderhughes, E. (1989). *Understanding race, ethnicity and power.* New York: The Free Press.

Rappaport, J. (1984). Studies in empowerment: Introduction to the issue (pp. 1-7). In J. Rappaport and R. Hess (Eds.), *Studies in empowerment.* New York: The Haworth Press, Inc.

Santamaria, M.C. (1990). Couples therapy: Analysis of a "praxis" with a Freirian perspective. *Family Process,* 29, 119-129.

Selvini-Palazolli, M., Boscolo, L., Cecchin, G., & Prata, G. (1980). Hypothesizing, circularity-neutrality: Three guidelines for the conductor of the session. *Family Process,* 19, 3-12.

Sheinberg, M. (1992). Navigating treatment impasses at the disclosure of incest: Combining ideas from feminism and social constructionism. *Family Process,* 31, 201-216.

Syme, S.L. (1986). Strategies for health promotion. *Preventive Medicine,* 15, 492-507.

Syme, S.L. & Berkman, L. (1976). Social class, susceptibility and sickness. *American Journal of Epidemiology,* 104, 1-8.

Tomm, K. (1987). Interventive interviewing. Part II. Reflexive questioning as a means to enable self-healing. *Family Process*, 26, 167-183.

Tomm, K. (1988). Interventive interviewing. Part III. Intending to ask lineal, circular, strategic and reflexive questions. *Family Process*, 27(1), 1-15.

U.S. DHHS Secretary's Task Force (1985). *Report on Black and Minority Health*, Volume I: Executive Summary, August.

Waldegrave, C. (1990). Just therapy. *Dulwich Centre Newsletter*, 1, 5-46.

Wallerstein, N. & Berstein, E. (1988). Empowerment education: Freire's ideas adapted in health education. *Health Education Quarterly*, 15(4), 379/394.

Walters, M. (1985). Where have all the flowers gone: Family therapy in the age of the Yuppie. The *Family Therapy Networker.* New York.

Walters, M., Carter, E., Papp, P., and Silverstein, O. (1988). *The invisible web: Gender patterns in family relationships*. New York: Guilford Press.

Weigarten, K. (1991). The discourses of intimacy: Adding a social constructionist and feminist view. *Family Process*, 30, 285-305.

White, M. & Epston, D. (1990). *Narrative means to therapeutic ends*. New York: W.W. Norton.

Zola, I. (1966). Culture and symptoms: An analysis of patients presenting complaints. *American Sociological Review*, 31, 615-630.

Violence in the Lives of the Racially and Sexually Different: A Public and Private Dilemma

Rhea Almeida
Rosemary Woods
Theresa Messineo
Roberto J. Font
Chris Heer

SUMMARY. This paper explores the dynamics of domestic violence in groups whose intimate experiences are most impacted by public forms of abuse and powerlessness, specifically heterosexual men of color and homosexuals of all races. Pertinent to this analysis are considerations of visibility and invisibility and the concepts of power and privilege. We suggest that feminist family therapy should view the public dimensions of abuse as a starting point for treatment conceptualization.

Rhea V. Almeida, ACSW, is Founder/Director, Institute of Family Services (IFS), 3 Clyde Rd., Suite 101, Somerset, NJ 08873. Rosemary Woods, MSW, is Assistant Director, IFS, Somerset, NJ. Theresa Messineo, MSW, and Roberto J. Font, MSW, are on the Faculty, IFS, Somerset, NJ. Chris Heer, MSW, is affiliated with Resource Center for Women and Their Families, Bound Brook, NJ.

The authors wish to thank Claudia Bepko, Robert Jay Green and Laura Markowitz for their extensive editorial support.

[Haworth co-indexing entry note]: "Violence in the Lives of the Racially and Sexually Different: A Public and Private Dilemma." Almeida, Rhea et al. Co-published simultaneously in the *Journal of Feminist Family Therapy* (The Haworth Press, Inc.) Vol. 5, No. 3/4, 1994, pp. 99-126; and: *Expansions of Feminist Family Theory Through Diversity* (ed: Rhea V. Almeida) The Haworth Press, Inc., 1994, pp. 99-126. Multiple copies of this article/chapter may be purchased from The Haworth Document Delivery Center [1-800-3-HAWORTH; 9:00 a.m. - 5:00 p.m. (EST)].

INTRODUCTION

Private, intimate violence occurs within the larger context of cultural violence. This 'culture of violence' is embodied by an implicitly hierarchical patriarchal structure that establishes certain patterns of subordination and oppression (Diagram 1). Intimate violence mirrors this more public violence. While the diagram is a simplistic representation, it provides a visual schema for larger group distinctions reflected in the larger culture. Because they operate on lower rungs of the hierarchy, women, heterosexuals of color, and homosexuals of all races[1] are impacted by the public violence of oppression in their private lives (Kivel, 1992).

Admittedly, enormous power differentials exist between poor, middle-class, and wealthy whites, Blacks, Asians, American Indians or Latinas/Latinos; however, a disproportionate number of people of color (heterosexual and homosexual) fall within lower socioeconomic levels (Almeida, 1993; Collins, 1989; Zinn, 1989). Where white working-class males might be oppressed daily by their wealthier white male employers, they generally are not as vulnerable to daily assaults due to the privilege of skin color and gender. These privileges place their oppression primarily within work environments. Furthermore, their gender and race provide them with cushions of freedom less available even to wealthy blacks or dark-skinned Latinos. Through their intimate connections with white men, white women also enjoy many privileges.

Inherent within the hierarchy of oppressions in capitalist society is the possibility of "passing" as a way of gaining privilege. Greene (1992) describes the social and physical desirabilities accorded to "white" or "light" skinned appearance that legitimizes "passing" at the cost of keeping invisible one's true identity. For example, a person of mixed Black and Italian heritage might choose to "pass" by publicly identifying with the white rather than non-white culture. Such choices of identification also can operate as within-group distinctions. Jewish women, for instance, might gain privilege by "passing" for gentile, at the cost of maintaining the invisibility of their heritage. These are some of the many survival strategies that those on the lower rungs of the hierarchy employ in order to gain access to the system of privilege erected by the dominant culture.

A major tool enabling oppression by the dominant patriarchal

Diagram 1

Hierarchy of Oppression

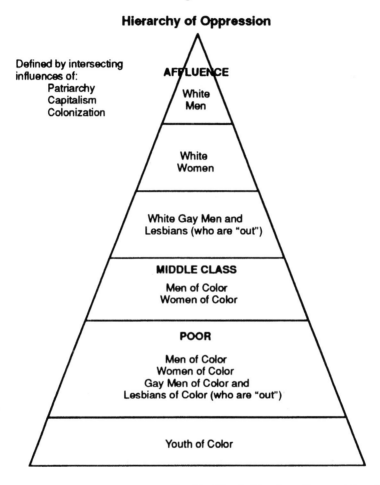

Defined by intersecting
influences of:
    Patriarchy
    Capitalism
    Colonization

AFFLUENCE

White
Men

White
Women

White Gay Men and
Lesbians (who are "out")

MIDDLE CLASS

Men of Color
Women of Color

POOR

Men of Color
Women of Color
Gay Men of Color and
Lesbians of Color (who are "out")

Youth of Color

Almeida, Woods, Messineo, Font and Heer (1993)

culture is that those in power, in this case white males, construct the
rules defining intimacy and the boundaries that differentiate the
public from the private. Women can be abused and suffer the effects
of male domination precisely because their roles as intimates of
men are defined as private ones. Social inequalities based on gender
create unequal social positions for women in their daily lives, con-

tributing to numerous psychological conflicts and devaluation of the self (Maracek & Hare-Mustin, 1991). Evidence of this oppression is visible in the large numbers of women over-represented in certain psychiatric groups (Greene, 1993; Cammaert & Larsen, 1988; Comas-Díaz, 1988). Locked within the boundaries of the nuclear family, white women have had little access to the public exposure that would empower them or provide them with assistance. Domestic violence against women in the heterosexual relationship has been kept secret–an unspoken "right" of the more powerful male. Attempts to make patriarchal oppression more public have met with intense resistance and backlash.

While privatization is the fundamental tool of patriarchal oppression within a white, heterosexual relationship (Almeida & Bograd, 1990; Avis-Myers, 1989; Bograd, 1984; Schecter, 1982), racial and homosexual oppression begin as public events (Almeida, 1993; Hurtado, 1989; Woo, 1985). Subjected to public displays of humiliation, marginalization, bigotry and hatred, the intimate relationships of heterosexuals of color and homosexuals of all races are undermined and rendered invisible by public policies and the absence of social supports. Domestic violence enacted in response to public violence often is used as evidence by the dominant culture to support notions of the "other's" inherent inferiority.

Lack of control over economic production keeps women and people of color in powerless and subordinate positions (Duneier, 1992; Comas-Díaz, 1991; Lorde, 1980). The process of colonizing "other" nations for valued resources and labor legitimates parallel processes of exploitation "at home." The dispossessed, or those who are rendered poor within the capitalist structure, are colonized[2] or "ghettoized." For instance, Lorde (1984) describes the public humiliation that Black men and women experience with respect to limited prospects for dependable work in a country with visible affluence. While violence by men of color towards intimates tends to be an expression of male domination, this violence is inextricably bound with other political forces that create polarizations of power and powerlessness, visibility and invisibility.

Those who have access to gainful employment or other economic entitlements, as middle-class white males generally do, benefit from the power of visibility. This is not the case for men of color and homosexuals of all races. Men of color, for example, are positioned subordinately to white men even before they are considered for employment. Being subordinate in the public world limits options for privilege and survival at multiple levels. Whereas white homosexuals may choose to keep their sexual orientation invisible, and thereby purchase access to privilege, they often do so at tremendous personal cost. Their visibility or self-disclosure around sexual orientation places them in a subordinate relationship to the dominant culture. These social dynamics can be largely attributed to the interplay of patriarchy, colonization, and capitalism.[3] By publicly identifying and labeling a group, the dominant culture establishes a foundation for the public abuse of those marked "other." The "other's" status in terms of visibility and invisibility is then defined by the dominant class, as are the public and private issues central to oppression.

Feminist theory is largely responsible for accountability-based treatment models that have demonstrated lower recidivism rates in contrast to models that emphasize psychological pathology (Bograd, 1988; Gondolf, 1988; Avis, 1985; Ganley, 1981; Dobash & Dobash, 1979). However, feminist analysis of domestic violence within the context of family therapy theory has tended to examine primarily the private oppression of white women in families and to ignore the more public forms of abuse that contribute to domestic violence in the racially different (Almeida, 1993) or sexually different. This article's emphasis on the sociopolitical matrix recontextualizes family therapy's reliance upon intra-familial dynamics. As volumes of feminist literature posit, both the interior of family life and its larger sociopolitical embeddedness are part of the problem and solution.

HETEROSEXUAL CONTEXT FOR INTIMACY[4] AND VIOLENCE

Heterosexism limits intimate bonds between men and women to relationships within the nuclear family. Within the nuclear unit, patterns of domination shape family life for women. Their subordination is reinforced through recurrent experiences of invisibility for women in the private realm (Walters, Carter, Papp, & Silverstein,

1990; McGoldrick, Walsh & Anderson, 1989). For instance, "house-wives" do hours of work caring for their families within the privacy of their homes, but such work is not valued monetarily or recognized publicly. Going public affords such women visibility: Paid work or active community involvement provide a powerful response to op-pression.

Within the heterosexist context, intimacy among women is ac-ceptable as long as it does not have a sexual component. Intimacy between men, while acceptable in rituals of sports, work, and recre-ational activities, is seldom supported when it has emotional or sexual overtones. By defining what is publicly acceptable and intol-erable, the dominant culture structures and sanctions rules for inti-macy. These rules, however, often exclude the racially and sexually different. The extended family relationships pivotal to family life in many cultures are disregarded. The dominant culture assumes that everyone's ongoing needs and desires will be fulfilled within the narrow confines of a heterosexual relationship.

THE CONTEXT FOR INTIMACY
FOR THE RACIALLY DIFFERENT

Many social factors alter the experience of intimacy for the ra-cially different. Society's notions of ideal love and intimacy are represented by exclusively "white" ideals of beauty not possessed by the racially different. Images of the racially different are rarely associated with images of beauty and hence are only marginally connected to positive notions of intimacy. Intimate connections among the racially different are generally perceived as unstable and of different moral fabric than those of the dominant culture. Social-ly constructed standards of beauty, intelligence, and economic secu-rity are employed to deter the integration of racial intimacy. Interra-cial unions, for example, are publicly discouraged through societal prohibitions that associate racial visibility with inferiority.

For men of color, visibility through physical appearance alone contributes to their subordination and consequent objectification of themselves and their families. This objectification occurs through pejorative framing of their intimate and sexual connections. Promi-nent examples can be found in pornographic materials, which sensationalize the sexual organs of black men, and often represent the black woman as a sexual servant to white males. Just as racially different women have been the handmaids to white men (as in the history of the master-slave relationship), so too have men of color been used by white women to engage in sexual activity deemed "taboo." None of these relationships are acknowledged publicly, but they continue within privately oppressive situations. So the public image reinforced is one in which intimate connections between the racially different and among interracial couples are unhealthy, abnormal, and rare. This form of public control of private lives does not resemble forms of control in white heterosexual unions.

Much of the private lives of the racially different is neither affirmed nor protected by institutions of our society. Intimacy among partners as well as parents and children is continuously under public assault. The lack of access to economic resources creates a situation whereby men cannot fulfill the responsibilities of providing for their families as society says they should. While the messages of "how to be a man" are explicit in male socialization, the differences in accessible resources are less clear, creating an exaggeration of the male role in family life and often in public life as well. This is evident in the social evolution of gangs within inner cities–a violent response to a violent context.

The multiple rules of privacy protecting the families of white males provide specific protection to the partners, sisters, daughters, and mothers of white men. These rules of protective privacy do not extend to the partners, sisters, daughters, and mothers of men of color. So while men of color assume the same patriarchal rules of privacy to control women in the home, they are not entitled to the same privileges that come with being white in a western patriarchy. For example, Ahmed, a Trinidadian Black male referred for physically assaulting his wife, insisted:

> 'I must have complete respect in my house–my home is the only thing I own in this country.' Born and raised in Trinidad, a former British colony, Ahmed is the son of an indentured servant from India. The British, who were largely responsible for the indentured-servant market between India and the Caribbean, ensured complete cut-offs between these men and their

families. Ahmed came from the Caribbean to the U.S. for a better life, as many from third-world nations do. Having faced generations of colonization, he is now confronted with a new history of racism.

Treatment with Ahmed focused on his violence towards his wife by educating him about the dimensions of power and control within intimate life. Using the Sponsorship model (Almeida & Bograd, 1990), we emphasized male socialization patterns inherent in domestic violence to show Ahmed how the use of power in terms of money, sex, emotional stonewalling, isolation, and finally physical violence led to his taking what he believed was "rightfully his." In addition, Ahmed was shown clips from *Straight Out of Brooklyn*, a film that depicts a Black marriage in which the husband repeatedly strikes the wife. The movie emphasizes the degradation that the husband experiences daily at his job as a gas station attendant: He is called "lazy" and is even spat upon. Eventually, he loses his job. With a family to feed and a 14-year-old son that looks up to him, the husband finds himself without money to pay the rent or buy his son a winter coat. The film examines the multiple levels of abuse that occur in the outside world, exacerbate tension within the home, and heighten the husband's desire to be a "man."

While we continually challenged Ahmed's use of violence towards his wife during all-male group sessions, we also differentiated his experience in the public world from the experiences of "white" men. His sense of public integrity is restored as he is confronted about his violence. A white middle-class man in the same group would not be treated in the same way. His sense of privilege and entitlement both within and outside of the home would be challenged as a first stage of treatment. He might be shown clips from *Sleeping with the Enemy* or *The Great Santini*. His experiences related to family-of-origin victimization would only be addressed after his consciousness is raised with respect to racial privilege and male entitlement. By differentiating such experiences for men of color, treatment provides a context that validates the multiple realities of oppression encountered daily.

When racially different men experience multiple oppressions in their public life, they may try to exert control over women in the home. This frequently gets played out in the form of violence towards their partners. Ho (1990) describes the hazardous effects of racism and cultural values with regard to male violence in Asian families: "Asian values of close family ties, harmony, and order support the minimization and secrecy of family violence in the privacy of one's home" (p. 129). Therefore, the context of publicly imposed exclusions from power and privilege should be considered simultaneously with familial experiences, when working with domestic violence. Key factors for the therapist to consider when assessing the dimensions of violence within the interior of a racially different couple's life are:

1. *Economic:* Often relegated to low-paying positions offering no benefits and limited upward mobility, men of color are frequently the last to be hired and the first to be fired. Men and women of color are less likely to speak out in support of fair labor practices, for fear of losing their jobs or jeopardizing their chances for promotion.
2. *Sexual:* Historically, men of color have been represented as animals with mythical and "inhuman" sexual prowess. Similarly, women of color have been portrayed as "exotic." These images, rejected as signs of physical legitimate beauty, have been exploited and objectified in pornography.
3. *Perceptions of Family:* Children of color are often perceived as delinquent and are generally devalued based on their appearance or speech patterns, such as "black English" or "other" languages/dialects. School personnel may launch a child abuse investigation if a child is consistently late or unkempt, disregarding the possibility that the child might come from a single-parent household in which the parent works a night shift.
4. *Physical and Psychological:* Instances of police brutality and harassment are far more likely when the "suspect" is a man of color. Men of color are more often singled out for investigation at police road checks.
5. *Emotional Isolation:* The homes and family lives of men of color are frequently exposed to the intrusions of police, welfare, schools, and other public institutions. The dearth of positive role models and the negative representations of persons of color in the media all serve to reinforce the notion that "white"

culture is the "ideal" to which "other" cultures may only aspire. Values of diverse cultures are not respected.

The process of differentiating these aspects of public abuse from power and privilege for men of color is essential to defining the public context of violence. An illustrative case is that of Jim, a mixed Cherokee and African American man with copper-colored skin and semi-curly hair:

> Jim was referred for brutally beating his Puerto Rican wife; there is a restraining order. He has been referred before and has had two prior restraining orders. However, he did not follow through with treatment. Jim is a janitor. In response to questions about his work life, Jim tells us of the racial slurs that are usually hurled at him in the cafeteria, mostly by children, sometimes indirectly by staff. He speaks of the humiliation that his children face because of his job, and his concern over possible lay-offs. In response to questions about his family of origin and connections to Cherokee lands, he cries and speaks of only hearing stories about land his great-grandparents owned. His parents were moved off the land, and he will never be able to afford to buy land on a janitor's salary.

Jim's violence towards his wife was confronted while simultaneously identifying the multiple levels of public assault that he and his family experience daily. As with Ahmed, we showed Jim clips of film addressing male violence in the home and extrapolating salient aspects of power and control within the couple's life. We simultaneously explored films depicting violence enacted against Native Americans. While Jim's consciousness was being raised about his use and abuse of power in the home, he also recognized his pain in the stories examined.

A major factor in efficacy studies of domestic violence centers on accepting vulnerability as an essential part of confronting the power inherent in male socialization (Gondolf, 1985; Ganley, 1981). This demonstrates an altering of the rigid system of denial that many batterers cling to. This process is critical to assuming conscious and personal responsibility for the violence. For men of color, this demand for accountability in relation to intimate violence cannot occur within a context that fails to acknowledge their experience of public abuse.

CONTEXT FOR INTIMACY
FOR THE SEXUALLY DIFFERENT

Like the intimate lives of heterosexuals of color, the intimate lives of homosexuals of all races are not publicly acknowledged; rather, they are devalued. Society pathologizes forms of intimacy that do not replicate heterosexuality and excludes them from normative descriptions of connection and family life: the same-gender connection that gays and lesbians embrace makes them different.

Rules of privacy used to maintain the oppression of women are similarly used to maintain homophobic attacks in the public sphere. Tactics of power and control such as (1) economic exploitation, (2) sexual abuse, (3) triangulation of children, (4) physical abuse and threats, (5) emotional abuse and isolation, (6) loss of spiritual and religious freedom, and (7) loss of heterosexual privilege are used to maintain the social invisibility of homosexual lifestyles. Personal intimacy is objectified, as it is for heterosexuals of color, through public intrusion into multiple aspects of the private lives of homosexuals. Moreover, the public violence to which gays and lesbians are subjected often is experienced in addition to rejection by their own families, who might have internalized the ideals of heterosexism.

Homophobia[5] sanctions the invisibility of homosexual lifestyles, placing enormous pressure on the homosexual to maintain a semblance of "normal" intimate life. Issues such as who will pay the rent, how medical benefits will be supported, whether or not to have children, and how normal lifecycle transitions such as "weddings," "engagements," and/or "pregnancies" will be acknowledged can become stressful elements of a homosexual couple's life. These pressures, coupled with the need to combat homophobia through a systematic rejection of heterosexual standards of intimacy, maintain a secrecy around dimensions of power and control within homosexual relationships. If one or both of the partners recognize that they are exploiting the other for money or sex, for example, but are reluctant to identify overtly with what resembles heterosexual practice, they may tend to deny the problem until it manifests itself in the form of verbal abuse and physical violence. When the couple decides to acknowledge the problem, the next serious dilemma is finding a safe place to take it. Homosexual couples know the extent to which society will blame the problem on the homosexual lifestyle rather than on the imbalance of power that structures oppressive practices among intimates.

PUBLIC AND PRIVATE CONTEXT OF ABUSE FOR THE SEXUALLY DIFFERENT

The public context of oppression situates the private violence that some homosexual couples experience in their intimate lives. Key factors for the therapist to consider when assessing dimensions of homophobic violence within the interior of a sexually different couple's life are:

1. *Economic:* If "out," the homosexual risks losing his or her job. Few states provide legal protection of civil rights for gays and lesbians.
2. *Sexual:* Society views homosexual practice as a whole as abhorrent and abnormal. Sexual orientation is often pathologized by therapists. In particular, lesbians have historically been subjected to sexual abuse by heterosexuals. Abuse ranges from the eroticization of lesbians in pornographic magazines and movies aimed at heterosexual male audiences to the more physically violent rapes enacted to "make them straight."
3. *Triangulation of Children:* The privacy of homosexual parents can be infringed upon by social agencies. Many have difficulty in obtaining custody of their own children and/or have been accused of being poor parents or pedophiles. Accusations attacking the credibility of homosexual parenting persist, despite research showing that gay parenting in itself does not have ill effects on children (Kirkpatrick et al., 1981; Hitchens, 1980; Miller, 1979; Green, 1978). Through social myths of homosexual inadequacy, the children of gay and lesbian couples are triangulated in attempts to malign the integrity and maintain the invisibility of gay parents.
4. *Physical Abuse and Threats:* "Gay bashing" and other forms of physical violence have become inescapable trials to those

who pursue alternate lifestyles. In addition, gays and lesbians face the threats of being disowned by their families, arrested by police, or even "outed" by other homosexuals.[6] Homosexuals, like people of color, are not always legally protected from violence. In fact, findings from the Comstock Survey (Comstock, 1991) indicate that 73% of victims of *all* forms of Anti Gay/Lesbian violence did not report incidents to the police. Of the victims of color, 82% did not report compared to 72% of white victims who did not report. In response to *very serious* violence, 58% of all victims did not report; again the percentage of non-reporting was higher for victims of color than for white victims.

5. *Emotional Abuse and Isolation:* Homosexuals are subjected to name calling, pejorative language, exclusions, and rejections by heterosexuals. Lesbians are accused of being "man-haters," and gays are accused of hating women, both without consideration to the rich and complex connections they have with male *and* female friends and family members.

6. *Spiritual/Religious Alienation:* Organized religions generally view homosexuals as sinners. Most gays and lesbians are forced to abandon their religious traditions and are alienated from their spiritual heritages. Spirituality as a larger form of human interconnectedness is compromised for gays and lesbians. Religion has historically helped people define and punctuate major life stages through rituals and celebrations. Exclusion from religion can mean exclusion from spiritual resources that mark important milestones in the life cycle.

7. *Denial of Heterosexual Privilege:* In the heterosexist society, homosexual couples are offered no legal protection from violence, no legal marriage, no tax deductions, no joint insurance coverage.

Assumptions of heterosexuality enforce the invisibility of gays and lesbians (Herek, 1990). This invisibility allows gays and lesbians access to the same level of privacy and privilege afforded to heterosexuals–provided they remain "closeted." Thus, the price for privacy includes great psychological and emotional costs (Maylon, 1982; Berger, 1990; Clark, 1987). The cost of being "out" entails the loss of numerous heterosexual privileges, such as participation in the military, housing, maternity/paternity leaves, funeral leaves, medical decision-making for partners inheritance, family insurance coverage, and legal protection from violence, both in public and private life. These losses combined with other direct forms of public violence are sufficient to coerce many homosexuals into a position of invisibility by "passing," lest they become the next victim (Berk, 1990). Invisibility, then, as an expression of homophobia, is a form of public abuse in that it intrudes on the private lives of homosexuals by requiring them to be "secret." In comparison, for homosexuals of color, the expressions of homophobic abuse are compounded by the overriding influence of racism (Greene, in press).

For the sexually different, dimensions of abuse exist first in public arenas and often get mirrored in their private lives (Comstock, 1991; Herek, 1990; Hammond, 1986; Hart, 1986). The statistics reported in the Comstock study indicate a similarity among the experiences of the sexually different, the racially different, and battered women: without society's structural supports to maintain familial survival, their private lives are publicly vulnerable. With few safe public places to go, the homosexual couple must solve their problems within the privacy of home life. When "out," they sometimes can at least rely on the support of family and friends, although they remain vulnerable in the public world. In a heterosexual family, however, being homosexual can be exquisitely isolating.

DYNAMICS OF ABUSE: PUBLIC AND PRIVATE

In addition to the overlapping effects from the impact of homophobia in the public domain, homosexuals of color are vulnerable to attacks of racism that exist within the white homosexual community as well. The difference in relation to identity of self between white homosexuals and those of color lies in the prominence attributed to race. Thus, for homosexuals of color raised in the United States, self-definition may occur first by race and second by sexual orientation (Morales, 1990). The coming out process is different for homosexuals of color than it is for their white counterparts, particularly with respect to racial socialization.

The collective racial socialization available to other minority groups is not available to homosexuals as a group. African American and Latino/a children, for example, learn the process of "armoring" to better confront the racism they will encounter throughout their lives (Clunis & Green, 1987). Parents of color are supportive and protective of their children, as they fight for a common cause. An African American woman recalls:

> My mother would always remind me to be on my best behavior when I was out with my friends. She would say, 'You're not like your white friend Mary; you will not get away with anything, but a white girl will get off easy. Your punishment will be much harsher; black people are treated differently because of the color of their skin.'

Combating racism is a lifelong struggle aided by personal and familial histories of competence. Because of a lack of similar socialization, homosexual children who are exposed to expressions of prejudice and hatred may not be sufficiently "armored" to defend against psychological assaults. They may hear homophobic comments from family members about AIDS being a punishment from God, and about homosexuals being child molesters and perverts. Therefore, an adolescent's choice to disclose his/her sexual orientation can bear a high price to the internal self or may create a great deal of conflict in the family. Families may use a number of coercive and controlling measures similar to those employed in the public domain to maintain the gay or lesbian members' invisibility. For instance, a Latina mother reacted to her daughter's coming out by saying: "My whole life has been a struggle with trying to protect you from bad men. Maybe it is a punishment from God that I shall have no grandchildren."

Family rites and rituals support heterosexual privileges to the exclusion of their homosexual members. Often there is no family recognition of the gay or lesbian partner even when the couple is "out" to the family. It is not uncommon for parents to hope that their homosexual children eventually will meet and marry heterosexual partners. Formal recognitions of homosexual unions may be absent. Coming out within such an environment is a "choice" of contradictions, amidst multiple jeopardies of losing the protection of cultural community, and family life. Green (1992) explains how race as a dimension of power in the identification of self, transcends the effects of class, education, occupation, and religion.

In addition to widespread homophobia, gays and lesbians of color must combat racism from both inside and outside of their communities. Edward S. Morales (1990) points out:

> The multi-minority status makes it difficult for a person to become integrated and [acculturated]. Within the mainstream society, ethnic minority gays and lesbians experience prejudice and discrimination for their ethnic identity, as well as for their sexual orientation. In the gay and lesbian community the social values mirror that of the mainstream society in relation to their perception of ethnic minorities which includes negative stereotyping and prejudicial attitudes about ethnic and racial minorities. Hence, ethnic minority gays and lesbians experience discrimination for their ethnicity within the lesbian and gay community. In the ethnic minority communities the social norms and values concerning homosexuality foster homophobic attitudes and consequently gays and lesbians within the minority communities face disapproval and rejection. (p. 220)

Racial oppression occurring both from without and within the homosexual community often pervades the interior of intimate life. Consider the following dialogue between two men of color, Rudy and Tomas (Almaguer et al., 1992):

> Rudy: I personally don't have that 'candy store' experience because I've only been in relationships with white men. Not that many; I've tried to make them long-term. For me the attraction had a lot to do with coming from the barrio, from the poor side of town. My second lover was middle class, "white bread" all over, from Pasadena, and on his way up the socioeconomic ladder to privilege. My desire was not only to be middle class, but to be an upwardly mobile, middle-class white man and participate in middle class America that way. I'm not quite sure what to think about that now, but class definitely has something to do with it.

Tomas: It has to do with power and how we eroticize difference in a racist society. We are socialized into European standards of beauty, but our sexual attractions are mediated by
being at the bottom of the racial hierarchy. At the center of
power, at the very top, is the mighty whitey; the white male!
So, when it comes to experiencing homosexual desire, it's
easy to understand how it is mediated by our structural position in society. I mean, after awhile, who wants another field
hand like themselves! I want the master! The master's piece,
to be more specific. It's really a case of unadulterated colonial
desire, but we live in a world full of contradictions. The point
is, learn to work with them–and enjoy them. (p. 34)

This dialogue reflects the internalization of oppression that occurs
around dimensions of beauty, intimacy, and other privileges of race
and class. For a Latino man, having a relationship with a white
middle-class man can create the illusion of restructuring social inequities.

ABUSE IN THE INTIMATE RELATIONSHIP:
RESPONDING TO THE PROBLEM

Domestic violence literature offers little concerning the impact of
public violence on the private context of homosexual intimacy.
Authors generally describe intrapsychic attributes, intergenerational
legacies, and a combination of sociopolitical and familial interactions that contribute to intimate violence. Island and Letellier (1991),
for example, provide a comprehensive overview of different theories
on violence, and endorse a pathology model for violence among
intimates. They claim that traditional psychological theories offer a
better explanation for the batterer's intrapsychic profile within intimate relationships. These authors part from feminist theory in ex-
plaining violence as connected to power imbalances in gender socialization, as they believe that it does not fit the profile of all
American men. Furthermore, these writers believe that batterers
overuse the explanation of sex-role socialization as a legitimate
explanation for their violence, which limits their potential for assuming personal responsibility. In addition, they advocate for the
DSM-III-R classification of the homosexual batterer: "We want to

stop the violence, now, and if labelling the batterer as mentally disturbed will help to stop the violence, as we believe it will, then it should be done now" (p. 60). While Island and Lettelier encourage victims of domestic violence to take public action by involving the police and obtaining restraining orders, their conceptual definition of intimate violence is restricted to the intrapsychic realm.

Ned Farley (1992) incorporates family-of-origin histories as an important aspect of violence, viewing battering as a symptom of dysfunctional intergenerational family systems. Farley attends to cultural differences as another dynamic in domestic violence but does not punctuate race as a contributing factor of oppression, either within the public or private spheres. Other authors emphasize gender socialization, with its differential aspects of oppression (Kanuha, 1990; Leeder, 1988; Renzetti, 1988; Hammond, 1986; Hart, 1986, Pharr, 1986), describing the oppressive influences of patriarchy, racism, and homophobia that intersect with intimate life and create patterns of identification with the oppressor in private contexts. Kanuha poignantly describes these influences as they relate to lesbians:

> The triple jeopardy they face as women living in a sexist society, as lesbians living in a homophobic society, and as people of color living in a racist society forms a web of silence and vulnerability with very little protection. In this often times isolated existence, lesbians of color in violent relationships are further hidden due to the shame and fear associated with domestic abuse. (p. 176)

Kanuha links this experience of "triple jeopardy" to the multiple levels of oppression with which lesbians of color live.

Once the couple's embeddedness within the larger context of oppression is unravelled, the therapist can assess and account for violence among intimates within the interior of the relationship. For instance, with lesbians who are physically abusive, it is important to identify the varying patterns of abuse in their family histories and tease out the emotional connections and loyalties that contribute to the use of violence. As when dealing with men of color, it is crucial to ensure the victims' protection by establishing safety plans and holding abusers accountable for their actions, while acknowledging the simultaneous and devastating effects of public violence. For example, Susie and Mishi, a white (Swedish) and Japanese lesbian couple with a history of violence, described the Japanese partner, Mishi, as "better educated" and having a "higher income." She also was the initiator of violence. While Susie was out to her family and her co-workers, Mishi was not; she feared that her parents, who already viewed her as being too western, would be entirely shamed by her homosexuality and would cut her off. Susie feared using the women's shelter due to possible homophobic reactions by mostly heterosexual women. A safety plan was devised that included Mishi moving to a friend's house for the duration of treatment. In addition, a small circle of the couple's friends were included in the therapy until the violence, as well as the other dimensions of power and control abated. Within this newly constructed social context connections and legacies within the family were gathered to begin to understand the intra-familial experience of violence.

Feminist theory asserts that abusive heterosexual men should not be permitted to use therapy to focus on childhood abuses while they continue to be violent or intimidate their wives, as it feeds into their sense of entitlement (Avis-Myers, 1992; Bograd, 1992; Kaufman, 1992). Research on heterosexual battering clearly shows a relationship between the public use of restraining orders and the curtailment of private violence (Pence, 1983; Gondolf, 1985a; 1985b; Sonkin, Martin, & Walker, 1985). The privilege of growing up male in a patriarchal culture offers men a sense of entitlement that frequently can only be taken away in a public context. These same arguments seem legitimately applicable towards the homosexual batterer who continues to abuse his or her partner. The major difference, in our view, exists in the public-private distinction and its relationship to the power and privilege central to therapeutic interventions. Like heterosexuals of color, homosexuals of all races live in an antagonistic society and often experience hostility on a daily basis. In contrast, most white men who were abused as children are not exposed to daily abuse as adults. Thus, it is appropriate and important to simultaneously address the private and public assaults on the intimate lives of homosexual couples.

Patriarchy teaches that one group can have power and control over another group and that violence is often an acceptable way to exert that control. Hart (1986) writes about this socialization experience and its effect on lesbian relationships:

> Lesbians, like non-lesbians, often desire control over the resources and decisions in family life that power brings and that violence can assure when control is resisted. The same elements of hierarchy of power, ownership, entitlement and control exist in lesbian family relationships. Largely this is true because lesbians have also learned that violence works in achieving partner compliance. Further, lesbian communities have not developed a system of norms and values opposing power abuse and violence in our relationships. (p. 175)

Violence within homosexual relationships is kept secret or even denied by the homosexual community (Hammond, 1986). This may be a function of the need to maintain a sense of pride and integrity, and differentiate from the heterosexual community through the belief that gays and lesbians have overcome this obstacle. Benowitz (1986) describes this phenomenon clearly: "We say that we do not have to contend with power issues, that we know how to have egalitarian relationships. We believe we are somehow able to sidestep many snags seen in heterosexual relationships." These beliefs lead homosexual victims and perpetrators to keep the violence private as a way of meeting that standard of ideal relationships. This ideal and sense of pride in their relationships is used to combat societal oppression, while paradoxically maintaining their invisibility.

Addressing violence in homosexual unions requires a reading of sometimes more subtle differences in power and privilege. Tracking these subtle imbalances includes the careful mapping of privilege based upon race, economics, household power, physical strength, gender roles assumed in specific areas of life, and the extent to which the couple is or is not "out." Because single incidents of physical abuse are not necessarily reflective of the overall pattern of domination in homosexual relationships, eliciting patterns of coercion and control are as relevant to therapy as obtaining information about physical violence. Hart (1986) suggests:

> Individual acts of physical violence, by definition, do not constitute lesbian battering. Physical violence is not battering unless it results in the enhanced control of the batterer over the recipient. If the assaulted partner becomes fearful of the violator, if she modifies her behavior in response to the assault or to avoid future abuse, or if the victim intentionally maintains a particular consciousness or behavioral repertoire to avoid violence, despite her preference not to do so, she is battered. (p. 173)

Since in homosexual relationships the wielder of power and control cannot be assumed as easily as it can in heterosexual relationships, the cycle of violence must be carefully tracked, as it was in the case of Susie and Mishi.

Within an interracial couple, the partner who can "pass" for white usually accrues more social power through his or her affiliation with the privileged majority. This often influences intimate relationships by mirroring the imbalance of power created in the societal context. When violence is initiated by the partner of color, therapy must first untangle the influences from the larger social system. Restraining the violence between the couple occurs simultaneously with validating any public attacks. This is similar to cases of female battering of men in heterosexual relationships with long histories of male coercion, domination, and battering that may have gone unacknowledged. The play of institutionalized entitlement in personal relationships can be subtle and difficult to identify. Societal influences that mythically separate the "personal" from "political" spheres of life provide limited consciousness regarding the insidious effect of living in a racist and homophobic society. This is especially distressing to partners who believe that their choice of an interracial or openly homosexual union comprises evidence of liberation and self-awareness. In such cases, there can be a high level of denial, as was evident in the case of a 30-year-old white middle-class male medical student involved with a black male law student. The law student assaulted the medical student physically. Therapy uncovered subtle forms of aggression on the part of the white partner, e.g., joking racist remarks about who should sign the lease if they choose to live together, how his lover's genitals were not as large as he first expected them to be, etc. The medical student did not view such comments as oppressive and insisted that his choice to be with his black lover was a reflection of his "openness." When working with an interracial couple, regardless of sexual orientation, the therapeutic unravelling of violence must include influences of the larger culture related to power and privilege.

CREATING NEW MAPS

Feminist family therapists do not perceive most violence as a personality disorder or physical/psychological pathology of some sort; instead, there is an emphasis on the analysis of male socialization with respect to power and privilege. Patriarchy varies in content and form for different men based on their location in the western world. An inclusive analysis of male domination must differentiate between resources and access to privilege.

Because there is no correlation between private and public violence for the majority of men who batter their partners (Avis, 1992; Gondolf, 1988; 1985; Ganley, 1981), treatment is conceptualized as an opening up of the interior dimensions of power and control. Treatment of the racially and sexually different has followed similar lines of analysis and solution. But there is a gross distortion in the analysis of power and privilege as they relate to men and women who are "different."

When addressing violence in racially or sexually different relationships, therapy must shift its traditional focus on the interior dimensions of power and control to the outer, public world as an initial point of reference. By using both levels of description–the outer, public world as well as the inner, intimate world–the therapist can name the violence and pull it out of the experience of a person's life. This type of larger framing includes stories about the racial, sexual, class and culture locations of their families over generations. Generational legacies are tracked within the larger context of oppression as described in the hierarchy of oppressions (Diagram 1). Victim-based models of accountability (Almeida & Bograd, 1990;

Gondolf, 1985) use the experience of the oppressed to expand the reality of the oppressor. These same strategies are used in working with the racially and sexually different.

To locate the power imbalance with a racially different couple, clinicians must take apart all aspects of privilege and power that maintain the interpersonal context. The following questions may help to do this:

- Who makes decisions regarding the spending of shared money?
- Whose name is on the bank accounts? Who makes more money?
- Whose time line has the couple been on in terms of dating, sex, decisions to live together?
- Who can more easily "pass?" Where and how?
- Who is modifying his or her behavior to avoid negative actions by the other partner?

In addition, when working with sexually different couples, the therapist might consider the following family of origin questions:

- Who makes decisions regarding how "out" the couple is?
- Who are you "out" to in your family?
- How did you choose the family members to tell?
- Have you experienced physical or emotional abuse due to your orientation?
- In what ways does your family support your relationship with your partner?
- What are some privileges granted to your heterosexual siblings not granted to you?
- Is your family aware of the violence in your intimate relationship? How have they responded?

Lastly, while the public illumination of private lives has proven to be a powerful experience of empowerment for white women trapped by intimate violence, it is less useful in authorizing the lives of heterosexuals of color and homosexuals of all races. The largely heterosexual public offers "legitimized" safety for the white heterosexual woman in a domestic violence situation (Rahman, 1989; Zinn, 1989). For her, the public world is less ambiguous. For heterosexuals of color and homosexuals, however, transforming the private to public, making the *invisible visible*, means confronting various public oppressions and privileges, while simultaneously relocating the dimensions of power and control. The therapeutic constructions offered herein embrace a collaborative context within which the dilemmas of the racially and sexually different are untangled. By bringing together the struggles of both the privileged and the oppressed, the compartmentalization of experiences through hierarchial separation is dislodged. Social and family agencies must stretch for relational initiatives that insert a level of safety within the center of public life, for many of these families remain on the fringes. This means not only expanding existing conceptions of therapy, but stepping outside of the therapist's office to forge alliances with community support structures friendly to families of color and homosexual families. To succeed in altering patterns of violence among intimates, we cannot attend exclusively to their private experience. Recognizing the degree to which experiences of oppression toward men and women of color, gays and lesbians normalize public violence is critical to eliminating violence within family life.[7]

NOTES

1. For purposes of the current analysis, the term "of color" refers to Blacks, Latinas/os (e.g., Chicanas, Puerto Ricans, Cubans), American Indians, Asian Americans (e.g., Koreans, Japanese, Chinese, Vietnamese, Filipino, and Indian), and those of mixed heritage who appear to be or identify with being "of color."

2. Colonized peoples in the United States are specifically American Indians, Blacks, and Chicanas/os; however, many immigrants share the experience of colonization.

3. For an analysis of such oppression, see Shiva (1988) and Duneier (1992).

4. "Intimacy" denotes human connections encompassing the sharing of love, affection, comfort, and security.

5. Pharr (1988) defines homophobia as "the irrational fear and hatred of those who love and sexually desire those of the same sex. . . . Like racism and antiSemitism, it is a word that calls up images of loss of freedom, verbal and physical violence, death" (p. 1).

6. "Outing" is the process of disclosing a person's sexual orientation to the public without the individual's consent.

7. Clinicians interested in obtaining instruments that may be shared with the client to identify the various distinctions of public and private abuse may contact the authors.

REFERENCES

Almaguer, T., Busto, R., Dixon, K., Lu, M. (1992). Sleeping with the enemy? Talking about men, race & relationships. *Outlook,* Issue 15, 30-38.

Almeida, R. and Bograd, M. (1990). Sponsorship: Men holding men accountable for domestic violence. *Journal of Feminist Family Therapy.* Vol. 2 (3/4), 243-256.

Almeida, R. (1993). Unexamined assumptions and service delivery systems: Feminist theory and racial exclusions. *Journal of Feminist Family Therapy.* Vol. 5 (1), 3-23.

Avis, J.M. (1989). Integrating gender into the family therapy curriculum. *Journal of Feminist Family Therapy,* Vol. 1, 3-26.

Avis, J.M. (1992). Where are all the family therapists? Abuse and violence within families and family therapy's response. *Journal of Marital and Family Therapy,* Vol. 18 (3), 225-233.

Avis, J.M. (1992). Current trends in feminist thought and therapy: Perspectives on sexual abuse and violence within families in North America. *Journal of Marital and Family Therapy.* Vol. 4 (3/4), 87-100.

Benowitz, M. (1986). How homophobia affects lesbians' response to violence in lesbian relationships. In K. Lobel (Ed.), *Naming the violence: Speaking out about lesbian battering.* Washington: Seal Press.

Berger, R. (1990). Passing: Impact on the quality of same-sex couple relationships. *Social Work,* Vol. 35 (4), 328-332.

Berk, R. (1990). Thinking about hate motivated crimes. *Journal of Interpersonal Violence.* Vol. 5 (3), 334-339.

Berrill, K. (1990). Anti-gay violence and victimization in the United States. *Journal of Interpersonal Violence.* Vol. 5 (3), 274-294.

Bograd, M. (1984). Family systems approaches to wife battering: A feminist critique. *American Journal of Orthopsychiatry,* Vol. 54, 558-568.

Bograd, M. (1986). Family therapy and violence against women. In M. Riche (Ed.), *Women and family therapy,* 34-50. Rockville, MD: Aspen Systems.

Bograd, M. (1988). How battered women and abusive men account for domestic violence: Excuses, justifications or explanations? In T. Hotaling, D. Finkelhor, J. Kirkpatrick & M. Straus, *Coping with family violence.* Newbury Park, London: Sage Publications.

Bograd, M. (1992). Values in conflict: Challenges to family therapists' thinking. *Journal of Marital and Family Therapy,* Vol. 18 (3), 245-256.

Bowen, M. (1978). *Family therapy in clinical practice.* New York: Jason Aronson.

Cammaert, L.P. & Larsen, C.G. (1988). Feminist frameworks for psychotherapy. In M.A. Dutton-Douglas & L.E.A. Walker (Eds.), *Feminist psychotherapies: Integration of therapeutic and feminist systems.* Norwood, NJ: Ablex.

Clark, D. (1987). *The new loving someone gay.* Berkeley, CA: Celestial Arts.

Clunis, D.M. & Green, G.D. (1988). *Lesbian couples.* Seattle, Washington: Seal Press.

Collins, P.H. (1989). A comparison of two works on Black family life. *Signs: Journal of Cultural Society,* Vol. 14 (4), 149-172.

Comas-Díaz, L. (1988). Feminist therapy with Hispanic/Latina women: Myths or reality? In L. Fulani (Ed.), *The psychopathology of everyday racism and sexism*. New York: Harrington Park Press.

Comas-Díaz, L. (1991). Feminism and diversity in psychology–The case of women of color. In *Psychology of Women Quarterly*, Vol. 15, 597-609.

Comstock, G.D. (1991). *Violence against lesbians and gay men*. New York: Columbia University Press.

Dobash, R.E. and Dobash, R.P. (1979). *Violence against wives: A case against the patriarchy*. New York: The Free Press.

Duneier, M. (1992). *Slims Table: Race, Respectability, and Masculinity*. Chicago: University of Chicago Press.

Farley, N. (1992). Same sex domestic violence. In Dworkin, Sari, Gutierrez (Eds.), *Counseling gay men and lesbians: Journey to the end of the rainbow*. Virginia: American Association of Counseling and Development.

Ganley, A. (1981). *Court mandated treatment for men who batter*. Washington, DC: Center for Women Policy Studies.

Gondolf, E. (1985). *Men who batter: An integrated approach for stopping wife abuse*. Homes Beach, FL: Learning Publications.

Gondolf, E. (1985). Anger and oppression in men who batter: Empiricist and feminist perspectives and their implications for research. *Victimology*, Vol. 10, 1-4, 311-324.

Gondolf, E. (1988). How some men stop their abuse: An exploratory program evaluation. In T. Hotaling, D. Finkelhor, J. Kirkpatrick & M. Straus, *Coping with family violence*. Newbury Park, London: Sage Publications.

Green, R. (1978). Sexual identity of 37 children raised by homosexual and transsexual parents. *American Journal of Psychiatry*, Vol. 135, 692-697.

Greene, B. (1992). An African-American perspective on racism and anti-semitism within feminist organizations. *Seventh Black International Cinema, Berlin*. Kino Arsenal, Welserstrade 25, 1000 Berlin 30.

Greene, B. (in Press). African-American lesbians: Triple jeopardy. In A.B. Collins (Ed.), *The psychology of African-American women*. New York: Guilford.

Hammond, N. (1986). Lesbian victims and the reluctance to identify abuse. In Lobel (Ed.), *Naming the violence: Speaking out about lesbian battering*. Seattle: Seal Press.

Hart, B. (1986). Lesbian battering: An examination. In K. Lobel (Ed.), *Naming the violence: Speaking out about lesbian battering*. Seattle: Seal Press.

Herek, G.M. (1990). The context of anti-gay violence: Notes on cultural and psychological heterosexism. *Journal of Interpersonal Violence*, Vol. 5 (3), 316-333.

Hitchens, D. (1980). Social attitudes, legal standards, and personal trauma in child custody cases. *Journal of Homosexuality*, Vol. 5, 89-95.

Ho, C.K. (1990). An analysis of domestic violence in Asian American communities: A multicultural approach to counseling. In L.S. Brown & M. Root (Eds.), *Diversity and complexity in feminist therapy*. New York: Harrington Park Press.

Island, D. and Letellier, P. (1991). *Men who beat the men who love them: Battered gay men and domestic violence.* New York, London, Sydney: Harrington Park Press.

Kanuha, V. (1990). Compounding the triple jeopardy: Battering in lesbian relationships. In Brown and Root (Eds.), *Diversity and complexity in feminist therapy.* New York: Harrington Park Press.

Kaufman, G. (1992). The mysterious disappearance of battered women in family therapists' offices: Male privilege colluding with male violence. *Journal of Marital and Family Therapy,* Vol. 18 (3), 233-245.

King, D. (1988). Multiple jeopardy, multiple consciousness. The context of black feminist ideology. *Signs,* Vol. 14, 1.

Kirkpatrick, M., Smith, L., and Roy, R. (1981). Lesbian mothers and their children. *American Journal of Orthopsychiatry,* Vol. 51, 545-551.

Kivel, P. (1992). *Men's work: How to stop the violence that tears our lives apart.* New York: Ballantine Books.

Leeder, E. (1988). Enmeshed in pain: Counseling the lesbian battering couple. Women and Therapy, Vol. 7 (1), 81-99.

Lorde, A. (1984). *Sister outsider: Essays and speeches by Audre Lorde.* New York: Crossing.

Lorde, A. (1987). Turning the beat around: Lesbian parenting. In S. Pollack and J. Vaughn, (Eds.), *Politics of the heart: A lesbian parenting anthology.* Ithaca, NY: Firebrand Books.

Maracek, J. & Hare-Mustin, R. (1991). A short history of the future: Feminism and clinical psychology. *Psychology of Women Quarterly,* Vol. 15, 521-536.

McGoldrick, M. (1988). Ethnicity and the family life cycle. In B. Carter & M. McGoldrick (Eds.), *The changing family life cycle–A framework for family therapy, 2nd Ed.* New York: Allen and Bacon.

McGoldrick, M., Walsh, F. & Anderson, C. (1989). *Women and families.* New York: W.W. Norton, Inc.

Morales, E. (1990). Ethnic minority families and minority gays and lesbians. In Bozett and Sussman (Eds.), *Homosexuality and family relations.* New York, London: Harrington Park Press.

Pence, E. (1983). The Duluth domestic abuse intervention project. *Hamiline Law Review,* Vol. 6, 247-275.

Pharr, S. (1986). Two workshops on homophobia. In K. Lovel (Ed.), *Naming the violence: Speaking out about lesbian battering.* Seattle: Seal Press.

Pharr, S. (1988). *Homophobia: A weapon of sexism.* Little Rock, Arkansas: Chardon Press.

Rahman, Q.A. (1989). Getting our house in order: Racism in the battered women's movement. *NCADV Voice.* Washington DC: National Coalition Against Domestic Violence, 1-2, 6.

Renzetti, C. (1988). Violence in lesbian relationships: A preliminary analysis of causal factors. *Journal of Interpersonal Violence,* Vol. 3 (4), 381-399.

Roth, S. (1985). Psychotherapy with lesbian couples: Individual issues, female socialization and the social context. *Journal of Marital and Family Therapy,* Vol. 11 (2), 273-286.

Schechter, S. (1982). *Women and male violence: The struggles and visions of the battered women's movement.* Boston: South End Press.

Shiva, V. (1990). Development as a new project of Western patriarchy. In I. Diamond and G.F. Ornstein, (Eds.), *Reweaving the world–The emergence of ecofeminism.* CA: Sierra Club.

Sonkin, D., Martin, D., & Walker, L. (1985). *The male batterer: A treatment approach.* New York: Springer.

Walters, M., Carter, B., Papp, P. & Silverstein, O. (1988). *The Invisible Web.* New York: Guilford.

Zinn, M.B. (1989). Family, race, and poverty in the eighties. *Journal of Women in Culture and Society,* Vol. 14 (4), 856-874.

Family Therapy:
Having a Place Called Home

Monica McGoldrick

SUMMARY. This paper discusses an Irish American woman family therapist's thoughts about culture, class, race, and gender in the context of family therapy. The difference in her power position as a woman and as a white person are described. The power politics of naming are discussed. The hidden dimension of class in a "classless" society is considered as are implications for family therapy training and practice.

I cannot be certain how far back in human history the habit of denial can be traced. All that I was taught at home or in school was colored by denial and thus it became so familiar to me that I did not see it. We keep secrets from ourselves that all along we know. The public was told that old Dresden was bombed to destroy strategic railway lines. There were no railway lines in that part of the city. But it would be years before the story came to the surface. I do not see my life as separate from history. In my mind my family secrets mingle with the secrets of statesmen and bombers. Nor is my life divided from the lives of others. I who am woman, have my father's face. And he, I suspect, has his mother's face.

–Susan Griffin: *A Chorus of Stones*

Monica McGoldrick, MSW, is Director, Family Institute of New Jersey, 312 Amboy Avenue, Metuchen, NJ 08840.

[Haworth co-indexing entry note]: "Family Therapy: Having a Place Called Home." McGoldrick, Monica. Co-published simultaneously in the *Journal of Feminist Family Therapy* (The Haworth Press, Inc.) Vol. 5, No. 3/4, 1994, pp. 127-156; and: *Expansions of Feminist Family Theory Through Diversity* (ed: Rhea V. Almeida) The Haworth Press, Inc., 1994, pp. 127-156. Multiple copies of this article/chapter may be purchased from The Haworth Document Delivery Center [1-800-3-HAWORTH; 9:00 a.m. - 5:00 p.m. (EST)].

Family therapy, like the other institutions of our society, has been structured in ways to support the dominant value system and keep invisible certain hidden organizing principles of our lives, including culture, class, race, and gender. Over the past few years I have been struggling, with the help of my colleagues, to see behind the blinders and understand what family therapy training and practice would look like if we could see more clearly. To explore this we must first examine the power of the defining values in our society.

THE MYTH OF THE AMERICAN DREAM

While the stated concept of our Constitution "liberty and justice for all" could open the door to a new world order, our society was, in fact, founded on exclusionary principles. On the surface we say that the "American Dream" is available to everyone, that with enough hard work and self-determination anyone can succeed. But the American Dream was not meant to be for everyone. We need to consider who it really is for, if we want to understand the problems our clients present to us, because our clients' pain often relates to their experience that their dreams cannot come true. Paradoxically, the ideals stated, but not meant, by our Constitution could be the foundation of a truly egalitarian human partnership society.

Our history books still brag about the foundation of our nation, minimizing the slaughter, slavery, and forced invisibility of more than half of the population. This is hard to see, because what we espouse overtly mystifies the underlying facts of exclusion. Everything we say falls at the intersection between the spoken and the unspoken. But our culture makes it very difficult to notice the unspoken or to hear the unsung voices. Our children memorize Abraham Lincoln's Gettysburg Address: "Four score and seven years ago our fathers brought forth on this continent a new nation conceived in liberty and dedicated to the proposition that all men are created equal." This excluded women, indigenous Indians, who were slaughtered to make way for the Colonists, who sought religious freedom for heterosexual white men, while African Americans were actually defined as 3/5 of a human being. The prominent myth that anyone can rise in class is, like the myth of gender equality and racial equality, a dangerous falsehood. To this day we are all–men, women, and children–paying for the mystification that our mythology of "Liberty, Equality, and Fraternity" creates. This mystification makes it almost impossible for us to see that our definitions of home, and family, and community are organized around systematic inequality. Maya Angelou, the African American poet, who traveled the world to look for home, since the U.S. felt so unhomelike, has written brilliantly of this search:

> The ache for home lives in all of us, the safe place where we can go as we are and not be questioned. It impels mighty ambitions and dangerous capers . . . Hoping that by doing these things home will find us acceptable or, failing that, that we will forget our awful yearning for it. (Maya Angelou, 1986, p. 64)

We need to transform our definitions of "home" and "family" so that they will truly allow us to be "as we are and not be questioned"– to feel safe and included and to have liberty and justice for all.

The mystification created by our pretense of "All men being created equal" makes it hard to think about the voices that are excluded. We have to revise our history books to make room for the mystified underside of the spoken–the unspoken secrets that structure the cultural, racial, class, and gender biased hierarchies, that are the underpinnings of our society. It goes unacknowledged that every 18 seconds an American woman is beaten by a man in her family, that African Americans are not represented in our institutions and do not have the same entitlements to participate even in our world of family therapy. It goes unsaid that anybody can *not* become President–not a woman, not a Black, not even a white man if he happens to be a Jew. It goes unsaid that where you come from does matter, that you can *not* shed your past, become whatever you want, or move up classwise just through hard work and desire.

We live in a society that is organized by disconnection and hierarchies. We are taught from childhood onwards to value success over empathy or attention to others' experience. By glorifying competition, war and violence in sports and entertainment, we are teaching our children that winning is everything, that a man is valued for his earning power, not his ability to be loving, gentle, or generous. He is also valued for his ability to "kick butt" and his sexual prowess, just as a woman is valued for her looks and her ability to ignore her own needs in favor of the needs of others. Thus we say we value motivation and hard work, but we really reward values like appearance, over which we have little control.

Many forces in our society press for disconnection through cut-offs of the "dangling ends" of past relationships that didn't work out, just as we cut off or ignore those who don't "fit in" with our culture's dominant values, such as the poor, the weak, the new immigrants, and the Native Americans, whose country we stole. These attitudes of denial, dissociation from what we don't want to see, and polarization of issues are all part of our press for simplistic perspectives–the 20 second sound byte, the black and white answers. In the world of psychology this type of dichotomous thinking leads to an over focus on solution–focused therapies before we have taken time for a meaningful definition of problems. It leads to splits between the mind and the body, the individual and the system, the nuclear and extended family, and dichotomizing here-and-now therapies from those that focus on the influence of the past.

THE MYTH OF THE AMERICAN FAMILY AS A SELF-SUFFICIENT NUCLEAR UNIT

Our entire society is organized to accommodate a type of family structure that represents only 6% of the U.S. population–nuclear family units with an employed father and a homemaker mother, who devotes herself to the care of her husband and children. Our entire business world and our entire educational system are organized for stay at home mothers and absentee fathers, even though the great majority of these wives and mothers are in the paid work force themselves. This means our society is neglecting the needs of our children for a full time protected, safe, stable environment watched over by caring adults. Our definition that two parents are critical for child development has always been a euphemism for a mother who is perpetually on-call for everyone emotionally and physically, and a distant money-providing father. Families with such a structure cannot help being problematic. I believe that fathering–like mothering–is forever. But it is not only because of the imbalance between father and mother in power and emotional role, it is also because this model ignores what seems crucial to the nurturance of families. There is much beyond parenting that is necessary. Children need more than 1 or even 2 adults to raise them, and these adults need more than 1 or 2 close relationships to get them through life. As family therapists we need to encourage our clients to go beyond the dominant culture's definitions of family–to pay attention to their relationships with their siblings, nieces and nephews, grandchildren, aunts, uncles. And beyond this, we need to attend to their friendships (especially for men), and to the health and safety of community context in which they find themselves. We need to help our clients repair their cut-offs not only from their parents but from their adult siblings. We need to consider the role of godparents, teachers, and other mentors in the rearing of children. We need the whole fabric of the family and community in order to raise children. As African Americans say: It takes a whole community to raise a child.

Unfortunately, this becomes virtually impossible when the society does not value the integrity of these relationships. Most family therapy, like our dominant social ideology in general, has tended to be oriented toward a view of families as traditional self-sufficient units, usually nuclear units. Made invisible in this perspective are all the families that are not organized in this way–about 94% of families in the United States. Poor families in the dominant view are seen as deficient, because they are obviously and critically dependent on systems beyond themselves for their survival. But we are all dependent for our survival on systems beyond ourselves and our nuclear families. It is just that those of us who are of the dominant groups fail to realize this, because we take the invisible ways the government supports us and our needs for granted. Schools, courts, the police, and all the other institutions of the society operate for the protection and benefit of the dominant groups. Thus, the dominant groups, who make the rules and definitions, are kept blind to their dependence on those who take care of them. So the real problem is not the dependence of certain people on the society, but the delusion of autonomy–that we of the dominant groups can use up the world's resources and not be held accountable; that we who are white can say we will let Los Angeles burn, because "They did it to themselves"–not realizing that "they" really includes us, and that, for example, our drug and gun industries and our prison system make money for the dominant groups in our society.

The experience of women, who have had to sacrifice their own needs and often even their lives for the "benefit" of traditional families remains invisible to the dominant groups in our society. Hidden from view are also all Americans who live in families that are not "traditional": those in three generational households, 2-pay-check families, gay and lesbian families, those poor enough to need public assistance, those whose housekeepers and child care providers are part of their functioning family system, and all other combinations of people who live in committed family relationships that are not part of the dominant view of a "normal" family.

THE POWER TO NAME

Generally speaking naming is done by those in power, which means that the issues of those *not* in the dominant group are obscured by their lack of power to give names to their experience. For example, the right to "Choice" and so many other issues of sexism have been defined as "woman's issues," rather than *human* issues, that affect everyone. Issues relating to people of color are defined as "minority issues," peripheralizing them by the very name "minority," but also conveying by the label that it is the job of people of color to solve the problems of racism, even though they have been invented and maintained by white society. The wounds of racism, like the wounds of sexism and classism, are problems of all of us. Our society's valuing of individualism, self determination, winning and autonomy makes it extremely difficult to realize the underlying connectedness of us all, and the price we all are paying for the inability of many in our society to have a voice or a name.

We in family therapy get paid by the names we gave to the problems our clients present to us. This naming is a powerful issue. An early 19th Century physician in the United States, Samuel Cartwright, described two mental disorders prevalent among slaves:[1]

1. *Drapetomania:* characterized by a single symptom: the uncontrollable urge to escape slavery.

2. *Dysathesia aethiopia:* for which many symptoms were described: destroying property on the plantation, being disobedient, talking back, fighting with their masters and refusing to work.

These diagnoses turned the desire for liberty into a sickness that was the problem of the slave, not the slave owner. Using labels to control others continues pretty much unabated even in family therapy. We are much readier to diagnose the victims of abuse than the abusers—we have our favorite acronyms MPD (multiple personality disorder), PTSD (post-traumatic stress disorder), SCS (survivors of child sexual abuse), defining the whole life course of those who have experienced trauma, but leaving out of our descriptions those who traumatize others, just as we did with slavery. The DSM-III-R, in the wisdom of its "scientific evidence" developed the diagnosis Self-Defeating Personality Disorder (301.90) to describe "those who choose people and situations that lead to disappointment, failure or mistreatment." Who are these people? We in family therapy have not spoken out against the overall family and community norms that make many of our labels a joke or a travesty. Traditional families are by their very structure dysfunctional, requiring the exploitation and dehumanization of family members, by requiring women to take care of the physical and emotional needs of others while ignoring their own, and requiring men to provide for the financial needs of others, while remaining on the periphery of the emotional life of their wives and children, with, however, the entitlement to abuse and neglect of others without society's sanctions for this.

Meanwhile, families of color, families of the poor, and immigrant families, whose norms and values are different from those within our naming scheme, remain peripheralized, invalidated, pathologized as deficient or dysfunctional, or, worse, invisible within our society. Many family therapists are still trained without reference to the insidious role that hierarchies related to culture, class, race, and gender play in the United States. They are taught concepts of human development, psychopathology, family functioning from the totally skewed patriarchal, classist, framework of the dominant white groups in our society.

BEYOND THE TYRANNY OF LABELS: MAKING ROOM FOR BOTH GROUP CONNECTIONS AND UNIQUENESS

Labels can be very reassuring and very dangerous because they define boundaries–who is in and who is out. Our labels of self-definition may be reassuring because they define a group to which we belong, thus overcoming our sense of isolation. But they also define the limits of that belonging. If we label ourselves "Woman, African American, Lesbian, Son, Brother, Schizophrenic, we are by those definitions Not-man, Not-Bosnian Muslim, Not-Heterosexual, Not-Daughter, Not-Sister. Coming to define myself as Irish American, for example, has been an affirmation at the deepest level of my belonging and my sense that neither I nor my family are alone in our ways of seeing the world–that much I thought was strange or eccentric I now see has a meaning because of our cultural history. At a certain point, however, by defining myself as "Irish American" or by any other fixed group identity, I may be emphasizing a certain exclusionary boundary, which distances me from others who are not Irish to whom I might better emphasize my connections.

Those in power have a hard time hearing from those who are disenfranchised. As Jean Baker Miller has described it so well, the disenfranchised know a whole lot more about those in power than those in power know about them, but they are systematically kept from being heard about what they know.

Virginia Satir once said, "We connect through our sameness but we grow through our differences." I believe that as a society we need to transform the way we think about definitions of sameness and difference. I believe our survival as human beings depends on whether we can remove the blinders of denial that prevent our seeing our human connectedness to each other. At the same time we must make more room to tolerate our differences. We must develop a perspective on our identity that allows for at least 3 levels of perspective:

(a) our common partnership with every other human being, without which we will surely perish
(b) our various group identities that give us a sense of home–of defining who we are in relation to others
(c) our uniqueness as individuals

Dealing with the subject of cultural diversity is a matter of balance between validating the differences among us and appreciating the forces of our common humanity. Each of us belongs to many groups. The sense of belonging is very important to our identity, but when the boundaries are overly enforced and the exclusion of outsiders becomes a primary definer of our group identity, it reflects something dysfunctional in the social system. It means that difference from outsiders rather than affiliation with group members is given prominence in our definition of our own identity. It means we are defining ourselves in the negative rather than in the positive.

We as family therapists should be working with our clients to develop multiple affiliate group identities, which increase the flexibility of their lives, to fit their ever evolving circumstances, rather than rigidly defined group identities with hardened boundaries that are constantly pulling at people's alliance, rather than helping them develop their potential on multiple dimensions. To do this we must expand our psychological theories of development to allow for the complexities of our identities with all their multiplicity. An excellent example of this complexity is described by the narrator, Vivian Twostar, in *The Crown of Columbus:*

> I belong to the lost tribe of mixed bloods, that hodgepodge amalgam of hue and cry that defies easy placement. When the DNA of my various ancestors–Irish and Coeur d'Alene and Spanish and Navajo and God knows what else–combined to form me, the result was not some genteel indecipherable puree that comes from a Cuisinart. You know what they say on the side of the Bisquick box, under instructions for pancakes? Mix with fork. Leave lumps. That was me. There are advantages to not being this or that. You have a million stories, one for every occasion, and in a way they're all lies and in another way they're all true. When Indians say to me, "What are you? I know exactly what they're asking and answer Coeur D'Alene. I don't add, "Between a quarter and a half," because that's information they don't require, first off–though it may come later if I screw up and they're looking for reasons why. If one of my Dartmouth colleagues wonders, "Where did you study?" I pick the best place, the hardest one to get into, in

order to establish that I belong. If a stranger on the street questions where (my daughter) gets her light brown hair and dark skin, I say the Olde Sodde and let them figure it out. There are times when I control who I'll be, and times when I let other people decide. I'm not all anything, but I'm a little bit of a lot. My roots spread in every direction, and if I water one set of them more often than others, it's because they need it more . . . I've read anthropological papers written about people like me. We're called marginal, as if we exist anywhere but on the center of the page. We're parked on the bleachers looking into the arena, never the main players, but there are bonuses to peripheral vision. Out beyond the normal bounds, you at least know where you're not. You escape the claustrophobia of belonging, and what you lack in security you gain by realizing—as those insiders never do—that security is an illusion . . . "Caught between two worlds," is the way we're often characterized, but I'd put it differently. We are the catch.[2]

Twostar offers here a brilliant expression of our multi-faceted identities—made up of the complexities of our heritage, our judgments about what is possible or preferable in a given context, and other people's projections onto us. She illustrates also the ambiguities that surround belonging, as well as what those who belong have to learn from those who are marginalized.

If we look carefully enough, all of us are a hodge-podge. Developing "cultural competence" requires us to go beyond the dominant values and explore the complexity of culture and cultural identity, not without values and judgments about what is adaptive, healthy or "normal," but without accepting unquestioningly our society's definitions of these culturally determined values. We should be working toward ways of considering our clients that allows them to stand in all their complexity, not having to suppress parts of themselves in order to "pass" for normal according to someone else's arbitrary standards. Home is about having a sense of being at peace with who we are. All of us are immigrants, always moving between the traditions of our ancestors, the worlds we inhabit ourselves and with our partners, friends and children, and the world we will leave to those who come after us. Probably no one ever has such a complete sense of connection to culture that there is no sense of disjunction ever, and for most of us finding out who we are culturally means putting together a unique internal combination of cultural identities.

The goal is to create a world we can each call home, a place where we will each have a voice where our flowing sense of group identities gives us more a sense of boundaries that include than of divisions that exclude, and where we will each realize our connectedness, knowing that none of us will really be free until all of us are free.

The notion of culture is almost a mystical sense of connection with all the threads of which our human community is woven. Paul Robeson, one of the most magnificent geniuses of our century or probably any other, wrote brilliantly of these hidden connections all of us have to each other, in describing one of his brothers, who did not live up to their father's expectations and eventually became involved in drugs and crime, before dying an untimely death:

> He won no honors in classroom, pulpit or platform. Yet I remember him with love. Restless, rebellious, scoffing at conventions, defiant of the white man's law. I've known many Negroes like Reed. I see them every day. Blindly, in their own reckless manner, they seek a way out for themselves; alone, they pound with their fists and fury against walls that only the shoulders of many can topple . . . When . . . everything will be different . . . the fiery ones like Reed will be able to live out their lives in peace and no one will have cause to frown upon them.[3]

If we appreciate this underlying connectedness, our therapy cannot just accept our clients' definitions of their problems. Their very descriptions reflect the prejudices that we all absorb from the dominant culture. No one is innocent or outside of the issues of sexism or racism or classism or other labeling, which results in the invisibility or oppression of anyone in our society. As Imelda McCarthy[4] has commented: "Clarity is the prerogative of the dominant group."

I believe we have to find a place to stand that holds each person accountable for his or her behavior, including intentional or unintentional sexism, racism or other unjust behavior. At the same time we must keep conveying a message of love and belonging that goes beyond the vicious acts anyone of us could commit. What this requires more than anything is our moving beyond our denial of our connectedness to each other.

MOVING BEYOND POLARIZATION: BLACK/WHITE, MALE/FEMALE, ETC.

It is very hard to discuss these ideas without discussion becoming polarized. We Americans have a great love of clarity about the good guys and the bad guys. We have to stay for the hard discussion. I used to think we could deal with sexism separately from racism, until my non-white friends taught me different. But we also can't deal with racism, while failing to acknowledge the sexism with which it is embedded. It is very hard for us to move beyond this. In fact, I would suggest that any time we think we are getting two opposites too clearly in focus, we should focus on a third perspective and see how the other two points look from there. For example, when we get too fixed on the difference between men and women, we might consider how those definitions might have to be reworked from a gay or lesbian perspective. Or, to break the "Black/White" polarization, we might explore these issues from a Latino or bi-racial perspective, and so forth.

There are two common pitfalls in discussions of diversity.

1. Discussion gets polarized particularly around the Black experience of white racism, leaving other people of color feeling invisible or excluded. Issues of sexism and homophobia are also pushed into the background in such a polarized context as people argue over which oppression is the worst or most important. This typically leads to the withdrawal of those who feel their issues cannot be heard or included in such a dialogue.
2. The second pitfall is to be so inclusive about diversity that it trivializes racism or leads to it being ignored in the multiplicity of other "isms." This often happens in discussions of cultural diversity, where proposals for inclusiveness are so extensive that they leave totally ineffectively addressed the primary institutionalized racism that is destroying our society.

Some issues are hard to raise in the context of other issues. The question of how one can address sexism with a couple who are themselves both victims of racism is a hot topic. The question of how to address the negativity about homosexuality within the African American community is also a hard topic to mention. I believe we need to keep a multi-dimensional perspective, which can at the same time highlight the overwhelming horror of institutionalized racism, while not making invisible other forms of oppression.

The multiple perspective I am urging means we must take into account the special invisibility of African American men and the particular way that racism has been directed against them, without ignoring the invisibility of African American women and the role African American men play in the oppression of African American women. We have to hold African American men accountable and at the same time understand the particular oppression they have been subject to for generations. While dealing with this, we must not humiliate or dehumanize white men, even as we must keep the pressure on them to be accountable for their privilege and entitlement. I have noticed that sometimes in discussions of diversity the "Black/White" issues predominate, leaving others feeling their issues have no place. The others then want to withdraw. We have to hold them in. We need each other–everyone.

DARING NOT TO ROMANTICIZE CULTURE

Even as we learn to appreciate cultural differences and the limitations of any one perspective, it makes no sense to say that just because a culture espouses a certain value or belief that it is sacrosanct. We must not move away from responsibility for the complex ethical stance required of us in our clinical work. All cultural practices are not equally ethical. Every intervention we make is political. We must not use notions of neutrality or "deconstruction" to shy away from committing ourselves to the values we believe in. We must have the courage of our convictions, even while realizing that we can never be too sure that the way we see things is the "correct" way. It means we must learn to tolerate ambiguities and continue to question our position and values in relation to the position and values of our clients.

For example, even as we must be rigorous in addressing racism, we must also deal with the oppression of women of color. It is not enough to blame it on white society, since patriarchy is deeply embedded in most of the cultures of the world, from Africa, to Asia and South America. I believe we must work for the right of every person to a voice, and a sense of safety and belonging. Those who would oversimplify the discussion must be called to task for their participation in silencing the voices of some in favor of the voices of others. This means that we must challenge those who say we should let cultural groups "speak for themselves," since that ignores the politics of who speaks for their group, which is probably, for most of the cultures of the world, a matter of patriarchal and cultural politics.

CLASS

The issues of gender, class and culture are interwoven in complex ways. Family therapists have recently been revising our theories through a new awareness of the role of gender in families. Culture is beginning to be inserted, though we have done less thinking about this. Generally we have left thinking about culture to minorities, as if the subject belonged only to them, and we do not consult them on anything else. At a political level we are most clear about the implications of gender in families. Class is the most toxic area of all. We operate on the myth that we are a classless society. Class is about power–who makes the rules and who has access to the resources. On the surface Americans tend to maintain that if class exists at all it relates to "the poor" as distinct from "us" in the middle class, or a little bit the upper class–which usually means someone else.

While you cannot change your gender or your culture, changing class is actually the expectation of our society. You may deny your gender or culture, you may not conform to stereotypic patterns of your gender or cultural group, but you cannot change who you are in these dimensions. Class is another matter altogether. Probably almost every family therapist has experienced class changes either themselves or within their families in the past generation. Because we change class by our money, our education, our occupation, or by marriage, we may end up in a class different from our parents, our siblings or our children.

We are all always–in every social context locating ourselves classwise–that is, defining who is above, who is below, and who is like us in class. But the problem is that we can't acknowledge this–therapists almost never talk about it. Changes in class, which are among the most profound social changes we experience, can generally not be talked about. Class differences may exist within the same family, making the experience of not being able to talk about them all the more painful. Siblings may end up in different classes, especially sisters, if they marry husbands from different classes, but also brothers, if their education or income is different. Parents and children may end up in different classes, if the children are upwardly mobile or if the children are disabled or retarded.

There is a hierarchical structure to culture and gender, but with class it's all about hierarchy, and it is denied, which makes it hardest to deal with. With gender and culture, there are aspects we can discuss in non-hierarchical ways. We can talk about differences between the values of men and women such as "his" and "her" ways of knowing, communicating, experiencing the world, as if there were no hierarchy–many people do. Much has been said about the male emphasis on autonomy vs. the female emphasis on context and relationship, as if these were equal but different values in our society. We can also talk about cultural differences in depoliticized ways though to do so means there is a lot we can *not* say. We can, for example, talk about the differences between Irish and Italians without discussion being polarized. But generally we cannot talk about the negative characteristics of any group but our own, except maybe to make fun of majority groups, criticizing WASP manners or German rigidity, for example. We can show preference of certain values over others (e.g., Irish dreaming over WASP work; Italian expression over Scandinavian stoicism), but it is harder to talk about differences in oppressed groups, because the differences are so often used for pernicious purposes of oppression.

With class there are even more taboos. Class is determined by a number of factors, one of which is money, which sets up an extremely dangerous situation. As Tom Wolfe says, if the "money nexus" becomes the primary determinant of class, as appears to be happening in our society, then all other ties and values, like kith and kin, are out the window. And this money nexus does seem to be taking over, as the devastating extremes between the "haves" and the "have nots" are dramatically intensifying year by year.

Education is another determinant of class, and we have a remarkably stratified system of judging class along school lines: from the Ivy League and the seven sisters colleges, to state universities, to community colleges, and so forth. Your occupation is another class indicator, and in our field one could lay out the stratification right across the board from M.D. to Ph.D., to Ed.D. or Psy.D. or D.S.W. to M.S.W. to M.A. to R.N. to B.A. to C.A.C. and so forth. Certain occupations may also take you out of the class you might otherwise be in according to your education and income, such as being a member of the clergy, an actor, or a politician. And then there is the question of what class you were born into, and what class you married into. A woman's class is usually determined by that of her husband. One interesting aspect of class is that unlike gender or ethnicity or race, which are matters of fact (though they may be denied), class, which is so profound a part of our interactions, is, to quite an extent, in the eye of the beholder. For example, if you are in a context in which one cannot tell your class, you may be related to as if it does not exist.

But class values enter all sorts of everyday activities such as what car you drive or even feel comfortable driving and what music you listen to. Opera, for example, defines your class, unless you're Italian, as does a penchant for Country and Western music. Your leisure activities also reflect class attitudes: golf or tennis mean one thing, bowling something different. There are also visible signs of a family's class in how they celebrate life cycle rituals, especially weddings. For example, the upper class and working class may go all out for a wedding. The upper-middle may see that as "gauche." What clothes do you wear as a therapist and how your office is furnished are all reflections of class, although this whole subject was never mentioned once in my training.

Class differences very often develop within families, as, for example, when a child is the first to have a college or professional education, which may create a painful chasm, because the loss created by the social distance cannot be acknowledged. The same is true for the class distance created in a family by a child who is downwardly mobile through severe disability or dysfunction. The inability to talk about the class distance makes it worse. Many people feel obliged to hide their origins in particular social situations, whether because they were poor or because they were privileged–out of fear that revealing their class background or even present class status would alienate them.

BACKLASH TO KEEP THE OPPRESSED INVISIBLE

In family therapy, as in every other structure of our society we see repeated efforts to silence the unheard voices who would speak up. For example, the family therapy field has for several years been reeling from the backlash of the feminist critique. Many men have withdrawn from professional meetings, saying the women are taking over, comparing women who speak out to "Darth Vader," suggesting that a single instance when a national family therapy conference had a predominance of women reflected the desire of women to "kill off" the men. Now as the issues of culture and race are beginning to be asserted, there is again fear expressed that "We better go slow, or the whites will retreat in droves from our organizations."

An example of this attitude is the letter by James Coyne[5] to the Family Networker in May of last year, criticizing and blaming working mothers, and in particular Betty Carter, for the invisibility of minority child care workers in American families. Coyne saw a picture of a white woman caring for her infant with the help of her minority child care worker as "a scathing indictment of the variety of feminism that is developing in family therapy." He went on to blame the ongoing racism in the family therapy field on the feminists, because, he said, it is they who are in the ascendancy in the field.

This kind of backlash indictment is typical of the forces aimed at silencing those without a voice in our society. Two groups who both have less power are pitted against each other, and the role of white males in maintaining the entire social construction is made invisible. Coyne chose to blame racism on the feminists. He did not even mention in his letter that the only article in that entire issue of the Networker (or in most other issues to date) to mention racism as a pernicious fact of our society and our field was Carter's. Throughout the Networker issue that Coyne wrote about were articles by white men that never mentioned racism or sexism, but Coyne chose to focus his lens on the one article that was trying to address the complex issues of oppression in American families. He also left undescribed both the laws that our society's white men have created which render it impossible for us to support and nurture our children or our poor.

Indeed, the issue of the Networker he was responding to reviewed the past 10 years of our field, but gave hardly a mention to feminism in several long articles, and did not mention racism at all. In the 10 year review, there were 90 authors quoted. Left unmentioned by Coyne was the fact that there was not one reference made to culture or racism in that review, nor that only 35 quotes or pictures out of over 100 about the decade were of women, and there was only a single quote from a person of color. Of course, Coyne is to be commended for mentioning the issues of racism at all, but it is most unfortunate that he does so only to blame another oppressed minority for them, thus perpetuating our culture's mystification of issues of oppression.

Of course Coyne's example of backlash is totally isomorphic to reactions at other levels of our society, where we are currently experiencing such serious backlash against any attempt to change the power hierarchy in American families.[6]

For example, the liberal press, including the Atlantic Monthly and the Utne Reader have recently published articles saying that the principal source of family decline over the past 3 decades has been the ascendancy of values "destructive of commitment, obligation, responsibility and sacrifice":

> The family has weakened because, quite simply, many Americans have changed their minds . . . about staying together for the sake of the children; about the necessity of putting children's needs before their own; about marriage as a lifelong commitment; and about what it means to be unmarried and pregnant.[7]

Hidden from view in this insidious paper is what it costs certain members of the family to keep the family going for everyone else.

Marriage for women has meant giving up their names, their identities, their right to privacy, their right to any control over how they spend their time—often their right to control over their own bodies. It has even often meant their right to their lives. Families have not been safe places for women or children in the American model. For example, during the Vietnam war, half as many women died by violence at the hands of family members as soldiers died in the war. In the U.S. today, more women are killed each year by their husbands, ex-husbands, and boyfriends than die of breast cancer or car accidents. Yet these losses and this violence go undescribed. This is a question of the right to name our problems.

The divorce rate in our country stands at 50%. According to the backlash of the media this leaves women depressed and children unattended to. But it is men who lose contact with their children after a divorce, not women. The average divorced father in the United States has a larger car payment than child support payment, and he is much more likely to keep up his car payment than his child support. Within a year after divorce 50% of fathers have virtually lost contact with their children. The world has recently born witness to our society's devaluation of our children as married women, such as Zoe Baird, but not married men, such as all the men in our governments, are being held accountable for our failure to create a society in which we value children enough to support them and their caretakers.

Virtually all the married women in our society of the current generation are being disqualified from public office because they hired illegal immigrants or women who work in an informal and poorly rewarded system that is not part of the official tax system of our society. Those who care for our children are among the most poorly paid workers in the culture. The men in our society are, by and large, seeing this as none of their business, even though it is they who write the laws that provide only a small fraction of the money for child care and education that they spend on the military. We pay our zookeepers and janitors more than our child care workers. Our entire social service system, which is generally staffed by poorly paid women to serve women and families, exists within an invisible context of a well-paid white male governmental system that controls the power, the money and the direction of services.

If issues of sexism have only surfaced in the field of family therapy in the past decade, concern about racism has been virtually absent from our discussion until the present time, which, again, is isomorphic to the way our dominant society has dissociated itself from dealing with racism in any meaningful way. Indeed, African American law professor, Derrick Bell,[8] has recently made the pessimistic prediction that our society will never move beyond our institutionalized racism, because it serves the dominant group's control. The top one million people in the United States make as much money as the next 100 million put together. As Bell has pointed out, if people realized their commonalties and shared interests across racial lines, it would create a revolution. So it is much safer for the dominant group to promulgate the myth that it is the Black man we really have to fear, rather than the power structure that holds our dominant class in place.

Bell's thesis highlights at a societal level the kind of attack Coyne made within our field in his attempt to turn people of color against white feminists, when the two groups have more in common than otherwise in their experience of oppression and invisibility in our society.

CHILD ABUSE AS A PRESERVER OF THE DOMINATOR MODEL OF HUMAN RELATIONSHIPS

Among the oppressions of American families that are implicitly structured into our hierarchical system, is child abuse, which is still the accepted belief within the dominant culture. This subject is almost never mentioned by family therapists either. Child sexual abuse, which, though disgracefully frequent, is much less frequent than physical violence against children, has become a "hot" topic in our field. But why do we not discuss physical abuse of children, which is so much more common? We know that abuse begets abuse. Those raised on ideas of domination and violence come to see it as a way to survive. Child abuse is protected by many of the dominant religions,[9] who hold to the adage: "Spare the rod and spoil the child," generally implying that this saying comes from the bible, which it does not. Our last President, George Bush, for example, grew up in a family in which beating a child with a belt was considered the way to raise a "gentleman":

> My father was a gentleman and he expected us to be gentlemen . . . If we acted disrespectfully, if we did not observe the niceties of etiquette, he took us over his knee and whooped us with his belt. he had a strong arm, and boy did we feel it.[10]

Family therapists need to pay more attention to the devastating impact of our violent culture on child development, and not ignore it just because our clinical families do not mention it themselves. It is a milestone that our current President acknowledges how horrific the physical abuse he witnessed in his own family was, and does not refer to it as helping him become a gentleman. In fact, we have just elected for the first time both a President and a Vice President who acknowledge having had family therapy. They are strong enough to acknowledge their vulnerability–their not always having the right answers or knowing how to proceed. But ideas such as acknowledging you need others' help, learning from your mistakes, and working toward consensus with others are not dominant in our society.

MARRIAGE AS A PRESERVER OF SEXISM, RACISM, AND CLASSISM

The institution of marriage is also deeply embedded in our patriarchal system, which institutionalizes the inequality of the sexes. No other relationship is so linked up with our very sense of who we are. For women marriage has generally meant the loss even of our names, not to mention our rights. I believe our mystification about "love" is essential to the preservation of patriarchy. The myth of Prince Charming is a most pernicious myth at the heart of the American Dream about families; according to this myth any couple can form the perfect American family, as long as she is white and beautiful, and not a lesbian and not disabled and is willing to give up her voice, her name, her class, and all other relationships for "him" and as long as he is also white, not gay, and not disabled, and has enough money to support her. The myth is that in striking their bargain, they will then live happily ever after. The myth is so appealing that it is extremely hard to give up.

In fact, marriage is the weakest relationship in the family–the only one which is not forever (as our divorce rate of 50% indicates); it is a paradox that this is the only family relationship we swear *is* forever. Indeed it would probably be a good idea if we made the promise to our parents, siblings, and our children to love them till death do us part!

Marriage is also the only family relationship where exclusivity is expected. We can love more than one child, sibling or parent. But we are not supposed to love more than one partner (at least not at one time). This too is linked to patriarchy, because the rule has always applied more to women than to men, a subject family therapists have only recently begun addressing. In thirty states it is still legal for a husband to rape his wife, it being against the law "to force a woman, not your wife, to have sexual relations."

Of course racism influences the ways sexism plays out in families in ways that make it impossible to consider one without the other. As Audre Lorde has written about differences between Black and white mothers:

> Some problems we share as women, some we do not. You fear your children will grow up to join the patriarchy and testify against you; we fear our children will be dragged from a car and shot down in the street, and you will turn your backs upon the reasons they are dying.[11]

TALKING ABOUT SEXISM AS A WOMAN, BUT RACISM AS A WHITE PERSON

I have experienced the difficulty of naming at a personal level from both sides of the power hierarchy. If I speak about sexism, men often give me a defensive response:

> She used to be so nice. What happened to her. She is accusing me. She hates men. She wants women to take over. Anyway, I didn't do anything. I didn't create the system. I'm not sexist

because I don't do anything mean to women. And besides, who is she talking about. I don't feel powerful.

It is not surprising that white men, even those who have the most power, usually do not feel powerful in our society, since it is based on a model of domination, competition and power hierarchies. White men, like all the rest of us, can never be sure of their power. There is always someone waiting in the wings for them to fail. No matter how successful they become, they are comparing themselves to others, who are even more successful, not to those who are below them in the hierarchy. Only if we shift our model to a society based on collaboration will we be able to free ourselves of these ways of thinking.[12] And the only proper definition of whether a man is sexist is not whether he actively discriminates against women or consciously oppresses them, but what he is doing to combat gender inequities that exist in our society and in his family and workplace.

There is the same problem in talking about racism, but here I fall on the other side of the power structure–the side of those with the power to define and name. And here it is I who find it hard not to do myself what I have seen men doing in response to the mention of sexism. It is very hard not to say:

Hey, why are you so angry. I didn't do anything to you. I had nothing to do with slavery or oppression. I'm not prejudiced, I'm a nice person. Racists are like the members of the Ku Klux Klan. How can you make that accusation against me? It's not my fault.

It seems that most white people's image of racism is lynching and other forms of overt cruelty, whereas when people of color use it, they are referring to things like not getting waited on as quickly as a white person or the unknowing, everyday micro-aggressions and insults that we who are white make through our ignorance of the experience or history of people of color.

In fact, it is even harder to deal with our racism because of the level of segregation that exists in our society. While men and women are, so to speak, "sleeping with the enemy," when it comes to racism, most whites in our society can dissociate themselves almost completely from awareness that the pain and rage of people of color is our problem too–not just their problem, because we as human beings are all in this life together.

DELIBERATELY NURTURING DIVERSITY

I think we should use the anger of the oppressed to help us stay attentive to our unintentional micro-aggressions. It can also remind us that we are part of the problem every time we are not part of the solution. This means: when we don't take responsibility for playing our part in overcoming racism, when we don't speak out to change things; when we don't attempt to overcome segregation by deliberately nurturing diversity in our lives; when we don't work to overcome our ignorance by learning the history of other races, which we did not learn in our childhood; when we don't attend to power inequalities and think twice before dismissing accusations of racism (even though they are hard to hear).

It is scary to think someone will call me a bigot or a racist or that I may be told "you just don't understand." Yet understanding is very hard, because there are so many entitlements I take for granted–such as not to be insulted when I walk into a store, an office, or just down the street.

But worse than our ignorance–which could be overcome by learning, is our inability to acknowledge our ignorance. The ignorance is reinforced by cultural rules that go beyond the ignorance a white therapist might feel from say an Afghanistani or Egyptian family, with whom it is possible to acknowledge our ignorance without guilt or the fear or censure. It is even hard for us who are white to acknowledge that we can't always understand the way Black people may speak. Just to admit that fact means we are racist.

I believe we must radically change our training to encourage white therapists to have the courage to jump over these barriers. We need to contend with this in order to become culturally competent family therapists. A first step is to acknowledge how "half-baked" we are. It will help to acknowledge our prejudice and to know that we will make mistakes–we will blurt out racist comments, will make micro-aggressions without realizing it. If we are lucky, someone will draw this to our attention and we will move along in overcoming our racism.

What we with our unearned privilege or power do not realize is how much we have to learn from those who have survived oppression. But the main point is that we are all in it together. Everyone is connected.

We need to expand ourselves to be open to appreciating other perspectives. To give just one small example, which has obvious implications for family therapy practice–the cultural style of African-American cultural groups tends to be organized in a circular fashion, in contrast to the linear organization of Western cultures.[13] Borneman suggests that a circular approach to music and language is a dominant feature of Black culture:

> While the whole European tradition strives for regularity of pitch, of time, of timbre, and of vibrato–the African tradition strives precisely for the negation of these elements. In language, the African tradition aims at circumlocution rather than at exact definition. The direct statement is considered crude and unimaginative; the veiling of all contents in ever-changing paraphrases is considered the criterion of intelligence and personality. In music . . . no note is attacked straight; the voice or instrument always approaches it from above or below, plays around the implied pitch without ever remaining on it for any length of time, and departs from it without ever having committed itself to a single meaning.[14]

In our dominant society there is a strong preference for a linear progressive organization, driving toward climax and catharsis (insight and relief tension); repetition is not valued.[15] When it occurs, it is employed for intensifying tension and there is a very strong demand for closure. By contrast, in African and African American cultures there is a circular organization with heavy emphasis on involvement through repetition of sound and movement. There is an episodic arrangement calling for small, short units leading to a succession of mini-climaxes. There is a retreat from closure in favor of the on-going and open-ended. In African American culture art is also not separated from "real life." In Euro-American society, there is a tendency to compartmentalize the arts, just like the tendency to compartmentalize subjects in education and to divorce them from aspects of everyday life.

ADDRESSING RACISM IN FAMILY THERAPY

Because these issues have been systematically obscured in our society, we as mainstream family therapists are part of the problem. Just as any man who is not actively working to overcome sexism is part of the problem, any white person who is not actively working to overcome racism is part of the problem. We who are white are ignorant about the lives of people of color, especially African Americans. Our education did not teach us about them. Our psychological theories did not include their experiences. We exist in segregated communities, where we do not usually run into them.

It might help to integrate in our training question about whether our trainees have ever had an African American friend, gone to see Black theater, read biographies of Black women and men, learned anything in school at all about Africa? The West Indies? The history of slavery? The history of Native Americans? Asian Cultures? The history of Latin America? It might help to encourage our trainees to discuss the fact that most of them live and have always lived in effectively segregated communities, gone to segregated schools and been educated not to notice the things we are describing here.

Peggy McIntosh, the educator, in her brilliant analysis of the phases of feminist re-visioning of curriculum, has set out for us some profound suggestions which could apply for all realms of education, including family therapy, and for all areas of oppression, including race, class, and culture as well as gender. She describes 5 phases. In the first phase we have womanless (minority-less) history.

Phase 2 considers women (minorities) in history. In this phase we expand our lens to include those special individuals who would make the cut, if we widen our lens somewhat, without altering our criteria for considering what makes history. We might then consider Frederick Douglas, Paul Robeson, Maya Angelou, Mary Cassatt, Julia Morgan, Marie Curie, Margaret Mead, and so forth. McIntosh considers this phase worse than Phase I because of the pretense of inclusion, when, by continuing to use the same definitions of value, it actually treats these "extra" people as "second stringers" in history. It conveys the message that women or minorities don't really exist unless they are exceptional by men's standards. As McIntosh puts it: "Women don't really exist unless we 'make something of ourselves' in the public world."

In Phase 3 we begin to describe women (minorities) as a Problem, Anomaly or Absence in History. In this phase we might consider the way history or biology has focused its lens in exclusionary ways, for example, using white males as the "normal" human body to be the subject of all American Medicine. Or we might consider that the "male gaze" is the perspective from which Western art is focused. We would notice that the male is prototype for human development in our psychological theories, and so forth. Erikson's 8 Stages of Man would be seen as related only to white men. The title of George Valliant's longitudinal study of several classes of Harvard students, *Adaptation to Life,* would need to be reevaluated, because it gave no indication of whose adaptation to which life. Books and presentations on family therapy would begin to be critiqued for the underlying limitations of their perspectives.

Phase 4 is about Women (Minorities) As History, taking the initiative to begin a redefinition of history and invent a history that does describe what women (minorities) have been doing. At this phase the definitions begin to break down as the boundaries between different spheres come to be seen as reflective of political assumptions. Academic disciplines as we have devised them might no longer make sense, because the hierarchy of values in terms of valued knowledge would be questioned. For example, the category of "Renaissance History" might no longer exist once one thought about the fact that neither women nor people of color had a renaissance during that period.

Phase 5 would be History Redefined or Reconstructed to include us all. McIntosh herself admits how hard it is even to imagine yet what this would look like, but surely knowledge would be a more interactive phenomenon. Learning a language, as she suggests, could be about more than the grammatical structure and the ability to speak or understand the language. It could include the ability to elicit information and feelings from others in the language, and to link it to previous conversations. She imagines a course in biology called "A Feeling for the Organism: Science Without Mastery," showing a revolutionary way of relating to our understanding the universe. In family therapy our categories for describing dysfunctional families might be radically transformed. Family therapists are notorious for obscuring in their descriptions of family patterns who did what to whom. We avoid terms like "men who batter their wives and children," transforming our language to obscure oppression in phrases like "violence in the family" and finally "violent families." Hopefully as we approach Phases 4 and 5, we will develop new ways of understanding relationships and our labeling will become more respectful of our families. Hopefully we will become less involved with language which pigeonholes others as we move beyond notions of mastering others. Obviously we have a long way to go. Currently being a "master family therapist" is the highest praise the American Association of Marital and Family Therapy gives to the field's leaders.

CONCLUSION

It is possible to develop a new societal organization that is neither patriarchal nor matriarchal, but based on the partnership of us all. Sexism is not a "women's issue," just as racism is not a "Black issue." The rights and freedom of each of us are the business of all of us. We will not any of us be free unless all of us are free. We will not any of us survive unless all of us can survive.

As a family therapist the implications of this in my daily practice are both obvious and obscure. Each day, with each intervention, if I am not part of the solution, them I am part of the problem. Getting clear about this is very difficult. T. S. Eliot has written:

> One has only learnt to get the better of words
> For the thing one no longer has to say, or the way in which
> One is no longer disposed to say it. And so each venture
> Is a new beginning, a raid on the inarticulate . . .[15]

I wish us all good luck in our new beginnings—our new raids on the inarticulate! We must be forgiving of ourselves for our difficulty seeing these issues clearly, for being "half-baked" and full of the old romantic ideas of patriarchy and cultural exclusion. And we must be rigorous in moving beyond these ideas or we will never make it.

NOTES

1. Discussed in Carol Tavris's *The Mismeasure of Women.* New York: Simon & Schuster.

2. Edrich, Louise, & Dorris, Michael (1991). New York: Harper & Row.

3. Robeson, Paul (1988). Here I Stand. Boston: Beacon Press, p. 16.

4. McCarthy, Imelda. International Family Therapy symposium, Amsterdam, Netherlands, May 1993.

5. Coyne, James (1992). The Family Networker, May-June.

6. Faludi, Susan (1991). *Backlash: The undeclared war against American women.* New York.

7. Whitehead, Barbara Defoe (1993). The new family values. *Utne Reader,* pp. 66-7, excerpted from Family Affairs (Summer 1992).

8. Bell, Derrick (1993). *Faces at the bottom of the well: The permanence of racism.* New York: Basic Books.

9. These ideas are brilliantly developed in Philip Greven's book: *Spare the Child: The Religious Roots of Punishment and the Psychological Impact of Physical Abuse* (Alfred A. Knopf, New York, 1990).

10. Quote from George Bush's brother Prescott Sheldon Bush, Jr., Greven, *Spare the Child,* p. 2.

11. Lorde, Audre (1984). *Sister outsider.* Freedom, CA: Crossing Press, p. 9.

12. Eisler, Riane (1987). *The chalice and the blade.* San Francisco: Harper & Row.

13. Borneman, Ernest (1959). Hale-Benson, 1982.

14. Borneman, Ernest (1959). p. 17.

15. T.S. Eliot (1934). *The Four Quartets.* In *Complete Poems and Plays.* New York: Harcourt, Brace & World, p. 128.

REFERENCES

Angelou, Maya (1986). *All God's children need traveling shoes.* New York: Vintage.

Bell, Derrick (1993). *Faces at the bottom of the well: The permanence of racism.* New York: Basic Books.

Borneman, Ernest (1959). *The roots of jazz.* In Nat Hentoff & Albert J. McCarthy (Eds.), *Jazz.* New York: Rinehart & Co.

Carter, Betty (1992). "Stonewalling feminism." The Family Networker, 16/1, January-February.

Coyne, James (1992). Letter to the editor on "Stonewalling feminism." The Family Networker, May-June.

Eisler, Riane (1987). *The chalice and the blade.* San Francisco: Harper & Row.

Eliot, T.S. (1934). *The Four Quartets.* In *The complete poems & plays.* New York: Harcourt Brace & World.

Erdrich, Louise, & Dorris, Michael (1991). *The Crown of Columbus.* New York: Harper & Row.

Faludi, Susan (1981). *Backlash: The undeclared war on the American woman.* New York: Crown.

Greven, Philip (1990). *Spare the child: The religious roots of punishment and the psychological impact of physical abuse.* New York: Alfred A. Knopf.

Griffin, Susan (1990). *A chorus of stones.* New York: Doubleday.

Hale-Benson, Janice E. (1982). *Black children: Their roots, culture, and learning styles* (Revised Ed.). Baltimore: Johns Hopkins Press.

Haskell, Molly (1985). "Women and Divorce." New York Times.

Lorde, Audre (1984). *Sister outsider.* Freedom, CA: The Crossing Press.

Miller, Jean Baker (1976). *Toward a new psychology of women.* Boston: Beacon.

Robeson, Paul. (1988). *Here I stand.* Boston: Beacon Press.

Tavris, Carol (1992). *The mismeasure of women.* New York: Simon & Schuster.

Valliant, G.E. (1977). *Adaptation to life.* Boston: Little, Brown.

Whitehead, Barbara Defoe (1993). "The new family values." *Utne Reader,* pp. 66-7.

Index

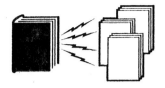

Haworth
DOCUMENT DELIVERY
SERVICE

and Local Photocopying Royalty Payment Form

This new service provides (a) a single-article order form for any article from a Haworth journal and (b) a convenient royalty payment form for local photocopying (not applicable to photocopies intended for resale).

- *Time Saving:* No running around from library to library to find a specific article.
- *Cost Effective:* All costs are kept down to a minimum.
- *Fast Delivery:* Choose from several options, including same-day FAX.
- *No Copyright Hassles:* You will be supplied by the original publisher.
- *Easy Payment:* Choose from several easy payment methods.

Open Accounts Welcome for . . .
- Library Interlibrary Loan Departments
- Library Network/Consortia Wishing to Provide Single-Article Services
- Indexing/Abstracting Services with Single Article Provision Services
- Document Provision Brokers and Freelance Information Service Providers

MAIL or *FAX* THIS ENTIRE ORDER FORM TO:

Attn: **Marianne Arnold**
Haworth Document Delivery Service
The Haworth Press, Inc.
10 Alice Street
Binghamton, NY 13904-1580

or FAX: (607) 722-1424
or CALL: 1-800-3-HAWORTH
(1-800-342-9678; 9am-5pm EST)

PLEASE SEND ME PHOTOCOPIES OF THE FOLLOWING SINGLE ARTICLES:
1) Journal Title: _____
    Vol/Issue/Year: _____ Starting & Ending Pages: _____
Article Title: _____
_____

2) Journal Title: _____
    Vol/Issue/Year: _____ Starting & Ending Pages: _____
Article Title: _____
_____

3) Journal Title: _____
    Vol/Issue/Year: _____ Starting & Ending Pages: _____
Article Title: _____
_____

4) Journal Title: _____
    Vol/Issue/Year: _____ Starting & Ending Pages: _____
Article Title: _____
_____

(See other side for Costs and Payment Information)

COSTS: Please figure your cost to order quality copies of an article.

1. Set-up charge per article: $8.00
    ($8.00 × number of separate articles) _____

2. Photocopying charge for each article:

    1-10 pages: $1.00 _____

    11-19 pages: $3.00 _____

    20-29 pages: $5.00 _____

    30+ pages: $2.00/10 pages _____

3. Flexicover (optional): $2.00/article _____

4. Postage & Handling: US: $1.00 for the first article/

    $.50 each additional article _____

    Federal Express: $25.00 _____

    Outside US: $2.00 for first article/

    $.50 each additional article _____

5. Same-day FAX service: $.35 per page _____

6. Local Photocopying Royalty Payment: should you wish to copy the article yourself. Not intended for photocopies made for resale. $1.50 per article per copy (i.e. 10 articles x $1.50 each = $15.00) _____

GRAND TOTAL: _____

METHOD OF PAYMENT: (please check one)

❑ Check enclosed   ❑ Please ship and bill. PO # _____
                     (sorry we can ship and bill to bookstores only! All others must pre-pay)

❑ Charge to my credit card: ❑ Visa;   ❑ MasterCard;   ❑ American Express;

Account Number:_____ Expiration date:_____

Signature: **X**_____ Name: _____

Institution: _____ Address: _____

City: _____ State:_____ Zip:_____

Phone Number: _____ FAX Number: _____

MAIL or *FAX* THIS ENTIRE ORDER FORM TO:

Attn: **Marianne Arnold**
Haworth Document Delivery Service
The Haworth Press, Inc.
10 Alice Street
Binghamton, NY 13904-1580

or FAX: (607) 722-1424
or CALL: 1-800-3-HAWORTH
(1-800-342-9678; 9am-5pm EST)